In music, **sight-reading**, also called *a prima vista*
(Italian meaning "at first sight"), is the practice of reading
and performing of a piece or song in a music notation that the
performer has not seen or learned before.

Wikipedia

THE EASY WAY TO SIGHT-READ RHYTHMS

by Kenneth Holmström

Originally published in Swedish as:
A Vista teknik, hur du blir en bättre notläsare, del 1 – Rytmbilder

© 1996, 2006, 2021 KHMP Förlag

ISBN: 978-91-972987-7-3

E-BOOK ISBN: 978-91-972987-8-0

DISTRIBUTION: BoD – Books on Demand, Norderstedt, Germany

Thank you! By avoiding illegal photocopying you are helping us
to keep on producing new material in the future.

CONTENTS

Chapter 8

Chapter 9

Chapter 10

Chapter 11

Chapter 12

Chapter 13

Chapter 14

Teachers guide

Study plan

Appendix

Introduction

Can you read this?:

"Aoccdrnig to a rscheearch at Cmabrigde Uinervtisy, it deosn't mttaer in waht oredr the ltteers in a wrod are, the olny iprmoatnt tihng is taht the frist and lsat ltteers be at the rghit pclae. The rset can be a toatl mses and you can sitll raed it wouthit porbelm. Tihs is bcuseae the huamn mnid deos not raed ervey lteter by istlef, but the wrod as a wlohe."

Chances are you could read it*. It is actually much harder to read it *exactly* as it's written! Try for yourself!

The text claims that the order of the letters inside a given word doesn't matter, as long as the first and last letters of each word are in the right place, and that you can read the words because the human mind reads words as a whole, and not letter-by-letter.

Well, that's what it says. But while it's entertaining and ego-boosting (that is, if you can read it), it isn't exactly so.

To begin with, this is actually **not** from a research at Cambridge University! According to Fox news[1], the text is from an e-mail that got viral and was originally sent around without mentioning Cambridge; it got added after the Times of London interviewed a Cambridge neuropsychologist for a comment.

Matt Davis, a senior research scientist at Cambridge University's Cognition and Brain Sciences Unit, spent some time tracking down the origin of this letter-transposition story. He found that it comes from a letter written in 1999 by Graham Rawlinson, a specialist in child development and educational psychology, to New Scientist magazine in response to an article written about the effects of reversing short chunks of speech.

Even if the text is not true to it's content, it is still a bit fascinating. Our brain has an amazing ability to sort out written information*.

The text above is not the only text that has gone viral. You can find several texts online on the same subject.

If you found the text above (or any text at all) to be very hard to read, you may have a language handicap (dyslexia). It's very common and dyslexia is known to affect approximately 5-8 % of the population.

Since reading music is strongly connected to our ability to read text you may also experience difficulties reading music.

---

[1] *https://www.foxnews.com/story/if-you-can-raed-tihs-you-msut-be-raelly-smrat*

Here is another text that's similar to those circulating the web. Here you find both mirrored letters and numbers making it even more unreadable:

15И'7 17 4M4Z1ИG 7H4T
Y0U C4И R34D 7H15 3V3И
7H0UGH 0ИLY 4
M1И0R17Y 0F 7H3
"L3773R5" 4R3 C0RR3C7?
1И 7H15 B00K Y0U W1LL
B3 U51ИG Y0UR 4B1L17Y
70 D3C0D3 P1C7UR35 –
RHYTHM-P1C7UR35
T0 B3 EX4C7.

Could you read it?

As it turns out, there was a rule. The substitutions were:
4=A; 3=E; 1=I; 0=O; 5=S; 7=T; and every N was written backwards.

So what has this to do with reading music?
Well, the thing is that musicians that read music well read music notes in the same way – by seeing the music as *pictures* or *words*, exactly as in written text, where we read *word-pictures*. The weird texts on previous page and on this page proves that this is the case.

In this book you will use this approach when learning how to sight-read rhythms and to speed up your reading.

You can use this book even if you've never read music before, and professionals can use it to enhance their reading skills.

If you are a beginner at reading music I suggest you use this book together with a music teacher.

The title of this book; "The easy way to sight-read rhythms" is of course a bold statement, but I do believe that this book is your shortcut to master the art of sight-reading rhythms!

I also urge you to follow the study plan at the end of the book to get a good learning progression.

Good luck!

Kenneth Holmström

Alingsås, Sweden
January 2021

CHAPTER 1

Eighth notes

Eighth notes

In this chapter we will explore eight rhythms that are *derived from four eighth notes*. Even if the chapter's heading is **Eighth notes** we will see other note values, but they all come from these four eighth notes. (You can find a list of note values in the Appendix, at the end of the book).

Here are the four eighth notes:

Let's call them **rhythm A**.

From these four eighth notes we can create another seven rhythms:
B, C, D, E, F, G and H. More on that later.

The goal is to see a rhythm as a whole (as a picture or word):

...instead of separate notes next to each other (letter-by-letter):

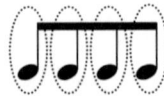

Reading rhythms well is largely built on the ability to see them as **pictures**.

Avoid "reading aids"

When learning how to read music you may encounter "reading aids" like "*1-e-an-a, 2-e-an-a, 3-e-an-a...etc*" to sort out rhythms, and they can be very useful. But in this book we avoid these as much as we can since they can be very confusing when you have advanced rhythms with **ties** and **rests**. (You will work with that later).

Here is a rhythm that could be difficult to say with that kind of reading aid:

See how complicated the reading aid becomes with advanced rhythms, if you want to follow it correctly.

> Instead, you can sound the rhythms in this book with any comfortable syllables that suit you. Like: *ta-ta-taa…* or *ta-ka-ta-ka-taa…* or *la-la-laa-la-va-la-va…* etc. You can, of course, also play the rhythms on a table, your knees or on your instrument.

If you sound the notes after a certain *system*, there will be several layers of concentration and that will make your sight-reading suffer.

Eight eighth note pictures

In the right column below, you see the eight rhythm-pictures (A-H) that we will study in Chapter 1.

These are all available rhythms that can be created from four eighth notes by tying together two or more notes with **ties** (a little bow between the notes), as shown in the left column below. The tie makes the note's duration longer. But we don't want to use ties if we can avoid it. Instead we usually write the rhythms as shown in the right column. (We will work more with ties later).

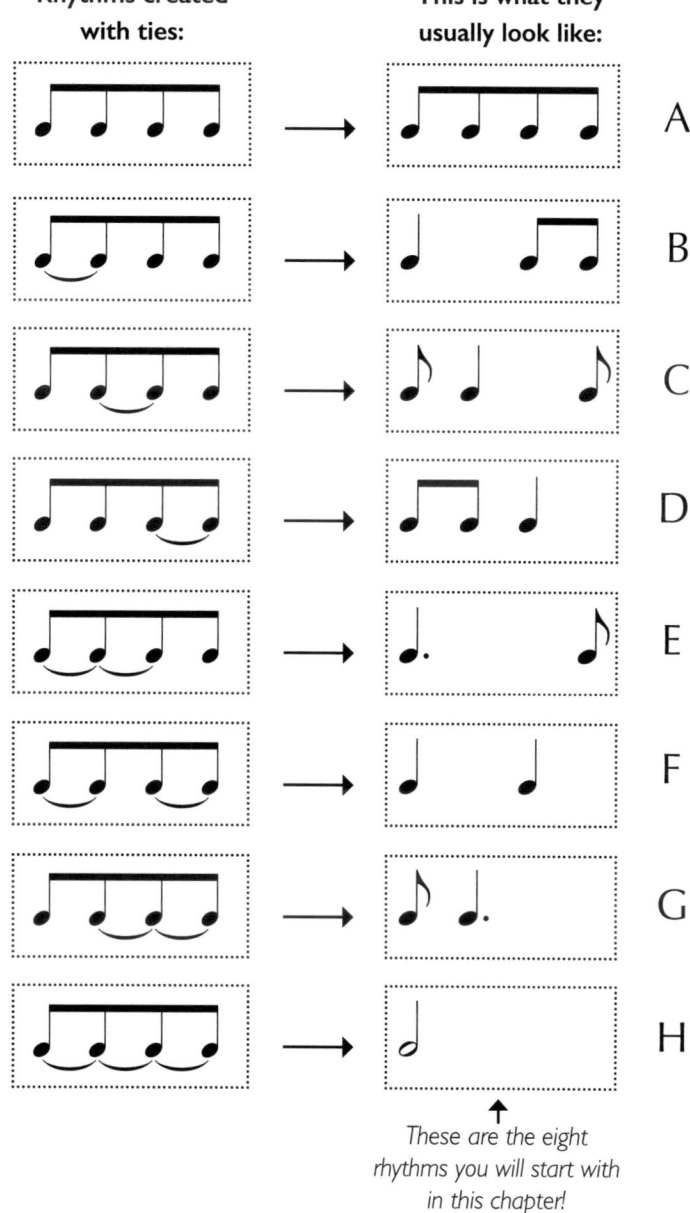

These are the eight rhythms you will start with in this chapter!

To take full advantage of this book's methodology, there are some important exercises that are vital for you to work with. They are called BASIC EXERCISES. You must really master them before moving on in the book!

You find the first **Basic Exercise** on the next page.

BASIC EXERCISE
1A

IMPORTANT EXERCISE

*Note: If you have little or no experience of reading music the **basic exercises** in this book are best learned with a teacher. They are meant to be a combination of learning **by ear** and **by sight**. Just as you would learn a new language, where you listen and repeat what the teacher says. You can also find the **Basic Exercises** with audio on our website: www.khmp.se*

If you already know how to read music you can study on your own. So this book can be used by both beginners and experienced students/musicians.

All rhythms in this exercise are in 4/4-time* and will span over two beats. The second half of the bar is made up of a **half rest** for two beats: ▬

This is what it looks like:

Start a metronome or a steady beat at approx. **80 BPM** (beats per minute).

1. Your teacher sings/plays **rhythm A** below. Student repeats. (While looking at the rhythm). Repeat this rhythm until you know it well.

2. Go to **rhythm B** and learn it in the same way as rhythm A.
    Listen and repeat.

3. Alternate between rhythm A and B.
    Don't forget the half note rest at the end of each bar.

4. Add the other rhythms one at a time until you have mastered all eight rhythms (A-H).

Remember to practice with a steady pulse.
(E.g. with a metronome or a person playing a steady beat).

Note:
See each rhythm
as a picture!

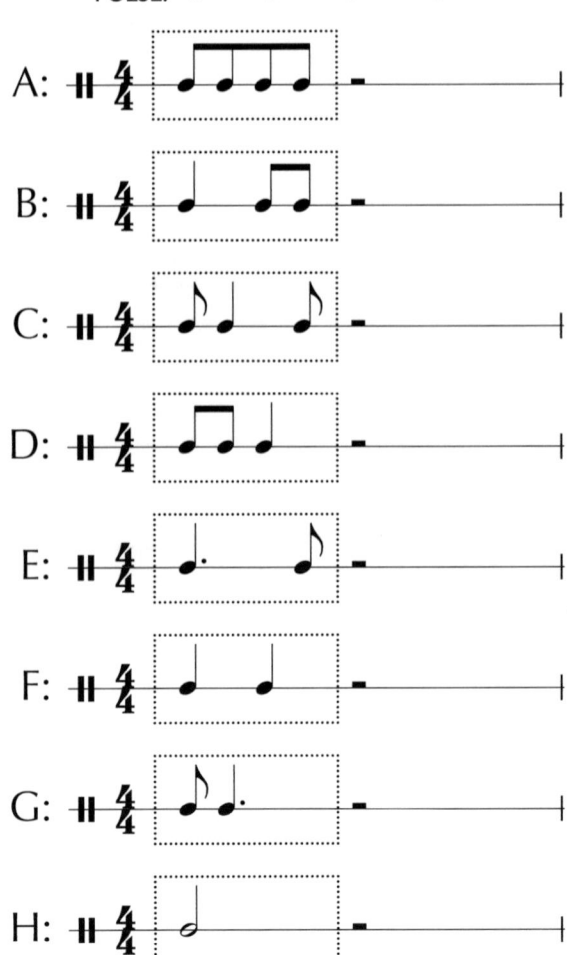

*You can read more about time signatures in chapter 11.

Make sure you know all eight rhythms (A-H) before you move on!

· ·

Let's fill a bar with rhythms

The next step is to combine the eight rhythms you learned in Basic Exercise 1A. We are going to continue with music in 4/4-time.

Imagine an **invisible line** in the middle of the bar, dividing it with two beats on the left side, and two beats on the right side. On each side of the invisible line you can put one of the rhythms you learned in Basic Exercise 1A. Like this:

On the following pages you will see an exercise that combines these eight rhythms in different combinations. Above each bar you'll see a letter combination. For instance: A.B. The first letter is pointing to the left side of the bar (two beats) and the second letter is pointing to the right side of the bar (two beats):

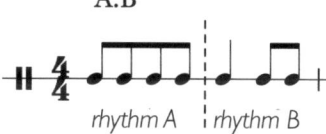

These letters have several functions. First, they tell us which rhythms are in that particular bar. Second, they help you or your teacher locate combinations that you are struggling with, or handle with ease, for that matter. Lastly they act as a guide for you to communicate with. Like:
Teacher: – Let's take it from D.E. (The letters are instead of bar numbers).

On the next page you will meet **Exercise 1a**. It presents all eight rhythms (A-H) in different combinations. You will have one rhythm in the first half of the bar and another (or the same) rhythm in the second half. *Divided by an invisible line in the middle, as mentioned above.*

It is important that you see each bar as two parts (two halves) or as two pictures! (To begin with).

Remember to practice with a steady pulse.
(E.g. with a metronome or a person playing a steady beat).

> ### Pro tip!
> *When playing/singing the first half of a bar you must try to look ahead to the second half of the bar at the same time. This will force your eyes to move forward and be prepared for what is ahead. When playing the second half of the bar your eyes should already be on the first half of the next bar, and so on.*
>
> *This is hard in the beginning but after a while you will master it. Start with half a bar and perhaps you can manage a whole bar or more in the future.*

Exercise 1a

Remember to divide each bar into two parts and see each rhythm as a picture.

Exercise 1a cont.

BEFORE YOU MOVE ON!

Before you move on in this chapter, which will develop the eight rhythms you have learned with **rests** *and* **ties***, I suggest that you jump to* **Chapter 2***. There you will learn eight new rhythms* **built from four sixteenth notes***. By doing that you will develop the ability to read rhythms derived from sixteenth notes in parallel with the eighth note based rhythms. Look at the* **study plan** *at the end of the book for a good progression plan.*

Rests (See also the Appendix)

When you read music it is important to know that rests are **active!** You can view them as **silent notes.** The notes' counterpart: **played silence!**

A rest in music doesn't always have to be written. The musician can choose to play a note shorter than noted and in that way create some space before the next note. *More on that on page 182.*

But now we will look at written rests.

Your goal is to see the rests as part of a bigger picture and that they belong together with the notes that come after:

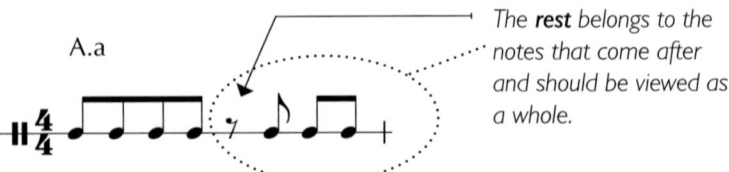

A.a

The **rest** *belongs to the notes that come after and should be viewed as a whole.*

Your next mission is to learn eight new rhythms. They are almost the same as in Basic Exercise 1A with the difference that **the first note** in every rhythm **is replaced with a rest** of the corresponding value.

If you have done Basic Exercise 1A thoroughly, it will be easier to manage the next step.

On to Basic Exercise 1B! ⎯⎯⎯⎯⎯⎯⟶

BASIC EXERCISE
1B
(RESTS)

IMPORTANT EXERCISE

You can find all Basic Exercises with sound on our website:

www.khmp.se

1. Start a metronome or a steady beat at 80 BPM (beats per minute).

2. Your teacher sings/plays **rhythm a** below. Student repeats. (While looking at the rhythm). Repeat until you master it.

3. Go to **rhythm b** and learn in the same way as rhythm a. Listen and repeat. (While looking at the rhythm).

4. Alternate between **rhythm a** and **rhythm b**. *Don't forget the half note rest at the end of each bar.*

5. Add one rhythm at a time until you have mastered all eight rhythms (a-h).

Remember to practice with a steady pulse. (With a metronome or a person playing a steady beat).

Be sure to know all eight rhythms before you move on to Exercise 1b on the next page.

Note:
See each rhythm as a picture!

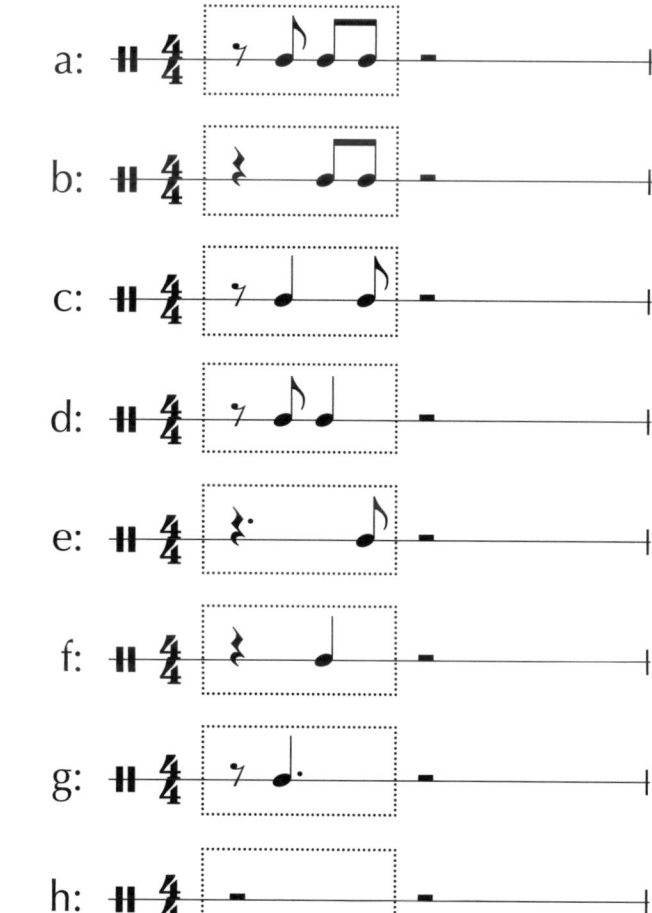

*Small letters above the bars in the exercises ahead, mean that the rhythm-pictures are modified with a rest (or a tie), while **capital letters** points to the original rhythm-pictures.*

Remember to divide each bar into two parts and see each rhythm as a picture.

Exercise 1b

Rhythm-pictures from Basic Exercises 1a and 1b.

Exercise 1b cont.

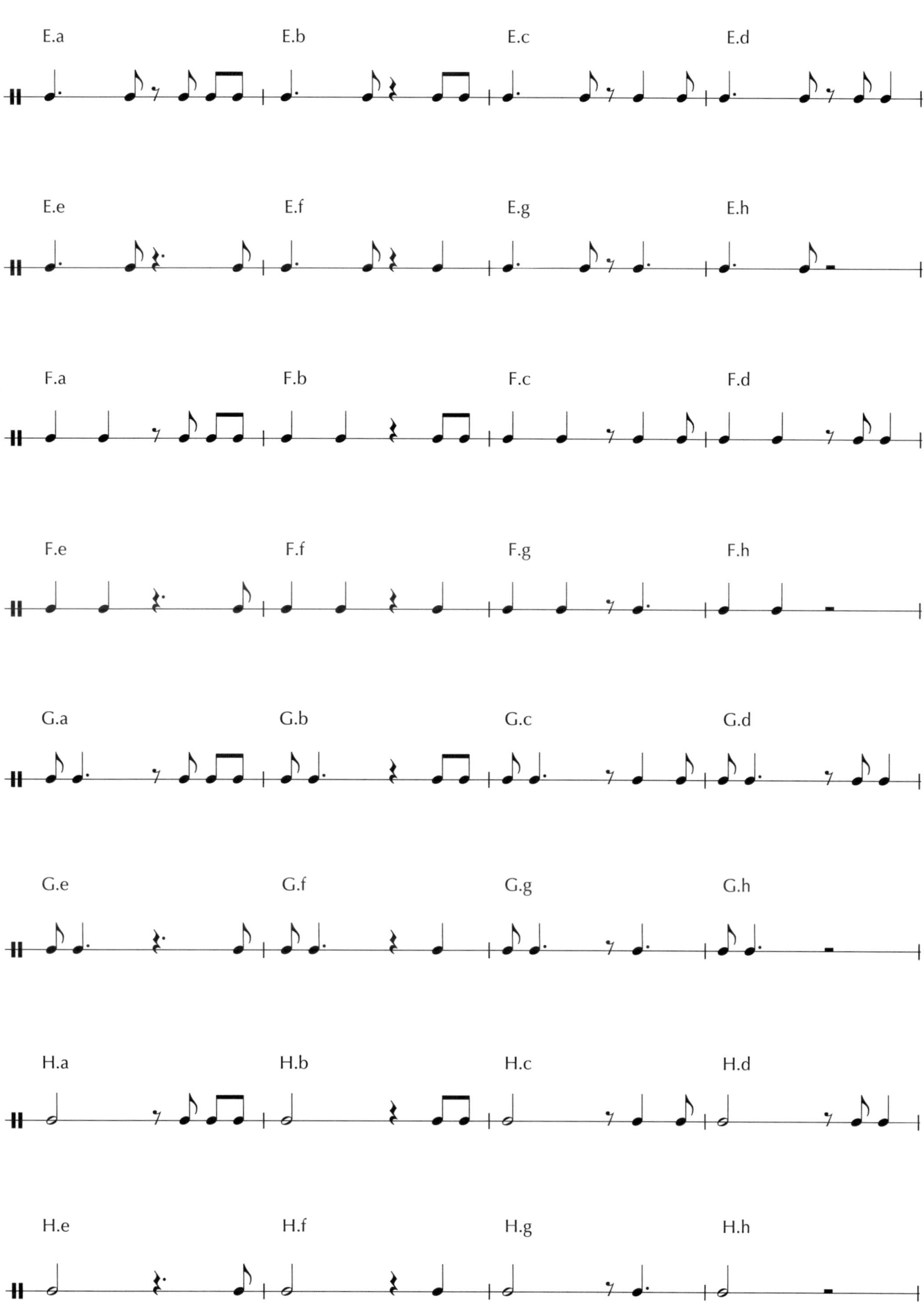

Ties

As mentioned earlier you can tie together notes (of the same pitch) to make them longer. Since it is more difficult to see a lot of ties we try to use other note values instead:

There are some exceptions. If the last note in a bar is tied together with the first note in the next bar you have to use a tie:

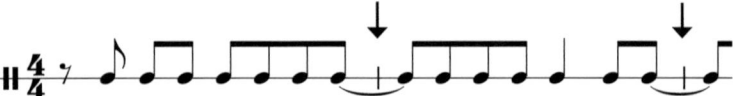

You should also do this with the **invisible line** in the middle of the bar. Think of it as a bar line (almost) and use a tie whenever a note must sound over this invisible line:

There are mainly three instances when to use ties:

1. When a note must sound over a bar line.

2. When a note must sound between rhythm-pictures within a bar.

3. To create (rare) rhythms.

The reason you choose a tie instead of a rest is probably because you want to make the note longer (obviously). Let's compare two rhythms:

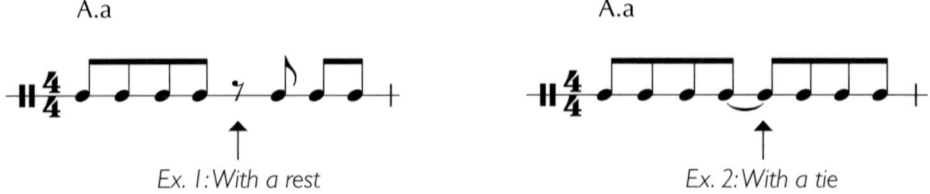

Note that the attack of each note is in the same place in both examples.

If you would play the examples above on a drum they would sound exactly the same since the notes' attacks are the same. Example 2 (with a tie) would have a longer sounding note in the middle if played on an instrument that can play sustained notes.

In a tie it is only the first note that has an attack. The following ("tied") note is just prolonged/sustained.

Here is the attack.

No attack, just sustain.

You will now notice that the tie in a way disturbs our rhythm-pictures from earlier. Suddenly the tie has glued two rhythms together making it sometimes more hard to read.

The first four notes sound exactly like **rhythm A** (from Basic Exercise 1A) but with the fourth note a little longer.

A.a

A.a

The second half is the same as **rhythm a** (from Basic Exercise 1B) since the attack of the first note is gone due to the tie.

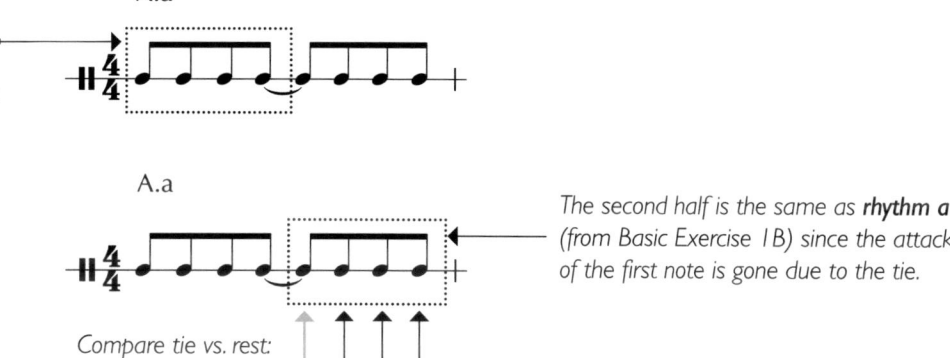

Compare tie vs. rest:

Ties and Rests

We will now develop the ability to read both ties and rests. On the pages that follow you will see rhythms from Basic Exercise 1A (A-H) and Basic Exercise 1B (a-h) but now with ties in some cases.

Go to the next page and do Exercise 1c. It uses ties between the two rhythm-pictures in each bar. *Please follow the study plan at the end of the book.*

Note: *If it is hard to play the whole exercise at once, you can split up the exercise by just playing one bar at a time or one row at a time, before you move on.*

TIP: *If you experience difficulties with ties you can try to mark the second note of the tie by for instance tapping your foot harder at the beat that follows the first note of the tie. (Also works with rests).*

C.a

Ex.

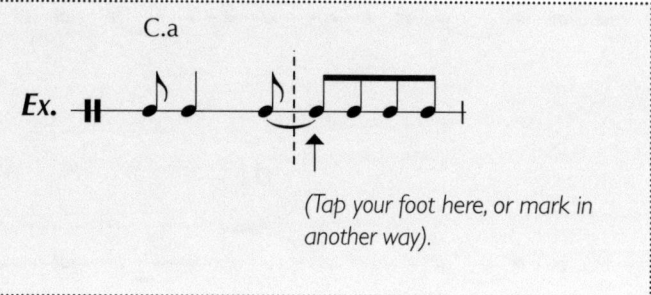

(Tap your foot here, or mark in another way).

Exercise 1c

Same as Exercise 1b but with ties instead of rests.

Exercise 1c cont.

Exercise 1d

Rhythms from Basic Exercise 1B and 1A.

Exercise 1d cont.

Exercise 1e

Same as Exercise 1d but with ties instead of rests.

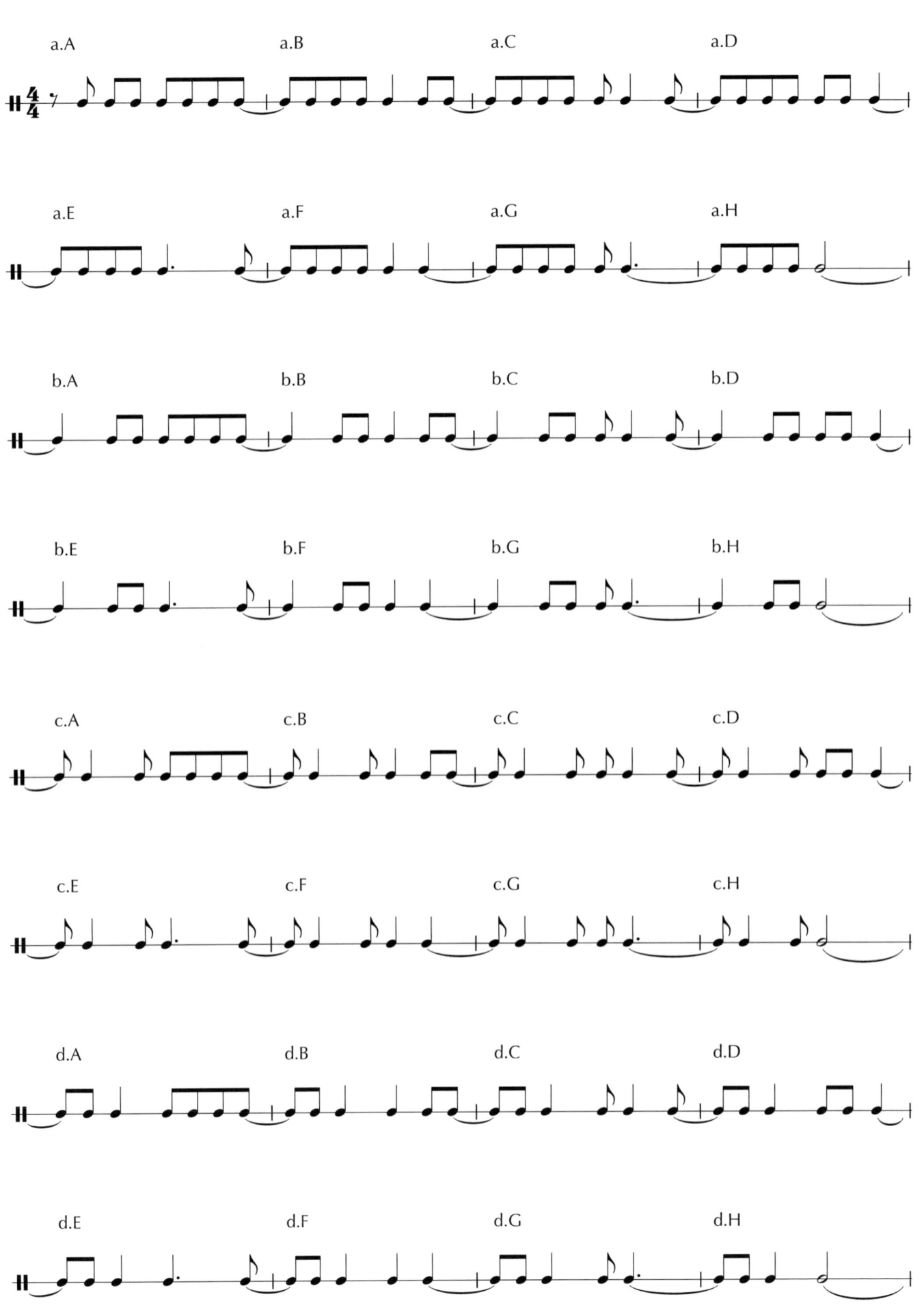

Exercise 1e cont.

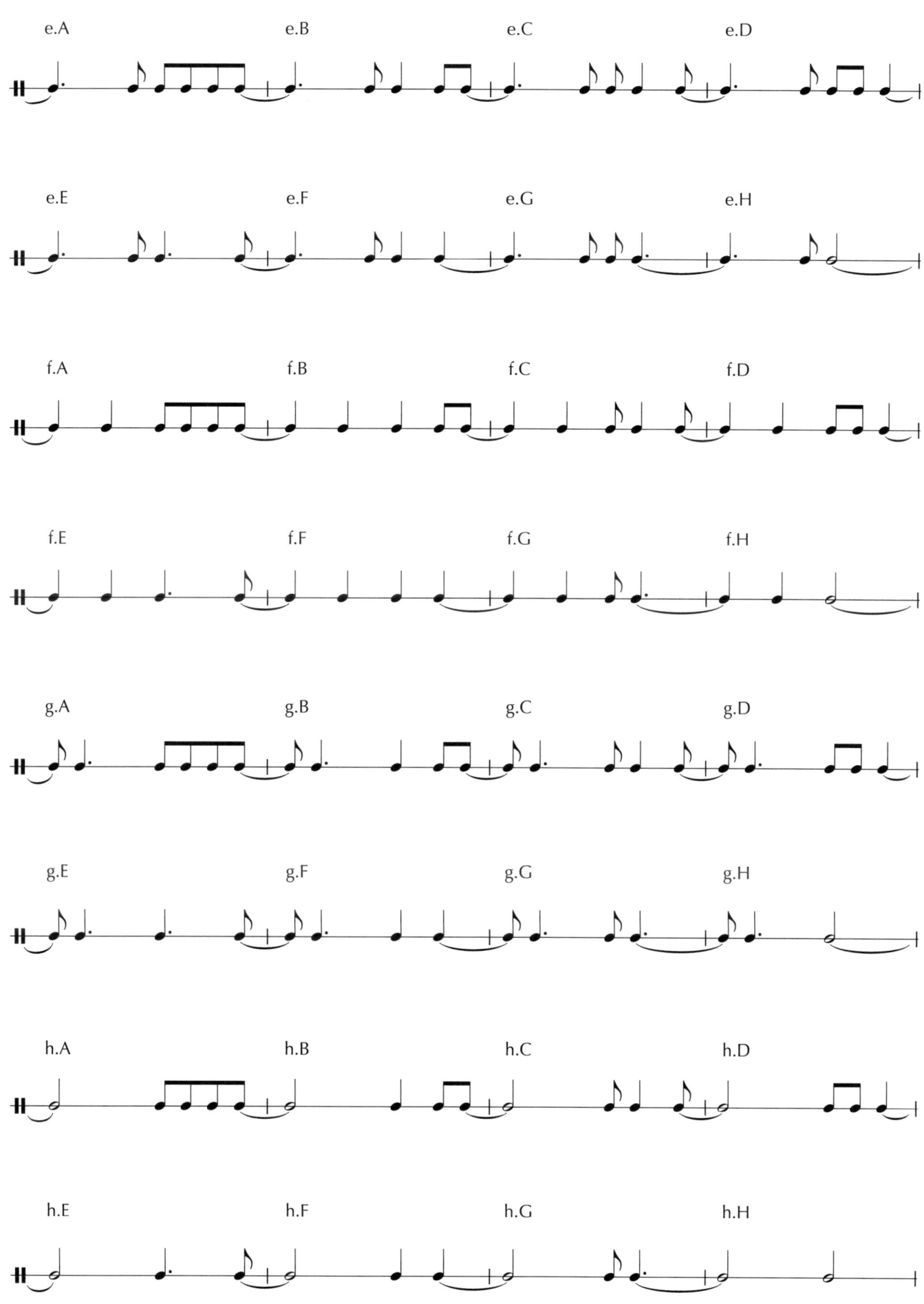

Exercise 1f

Rhythms from Basic Exercise 1B.

Exercise 1f cont.

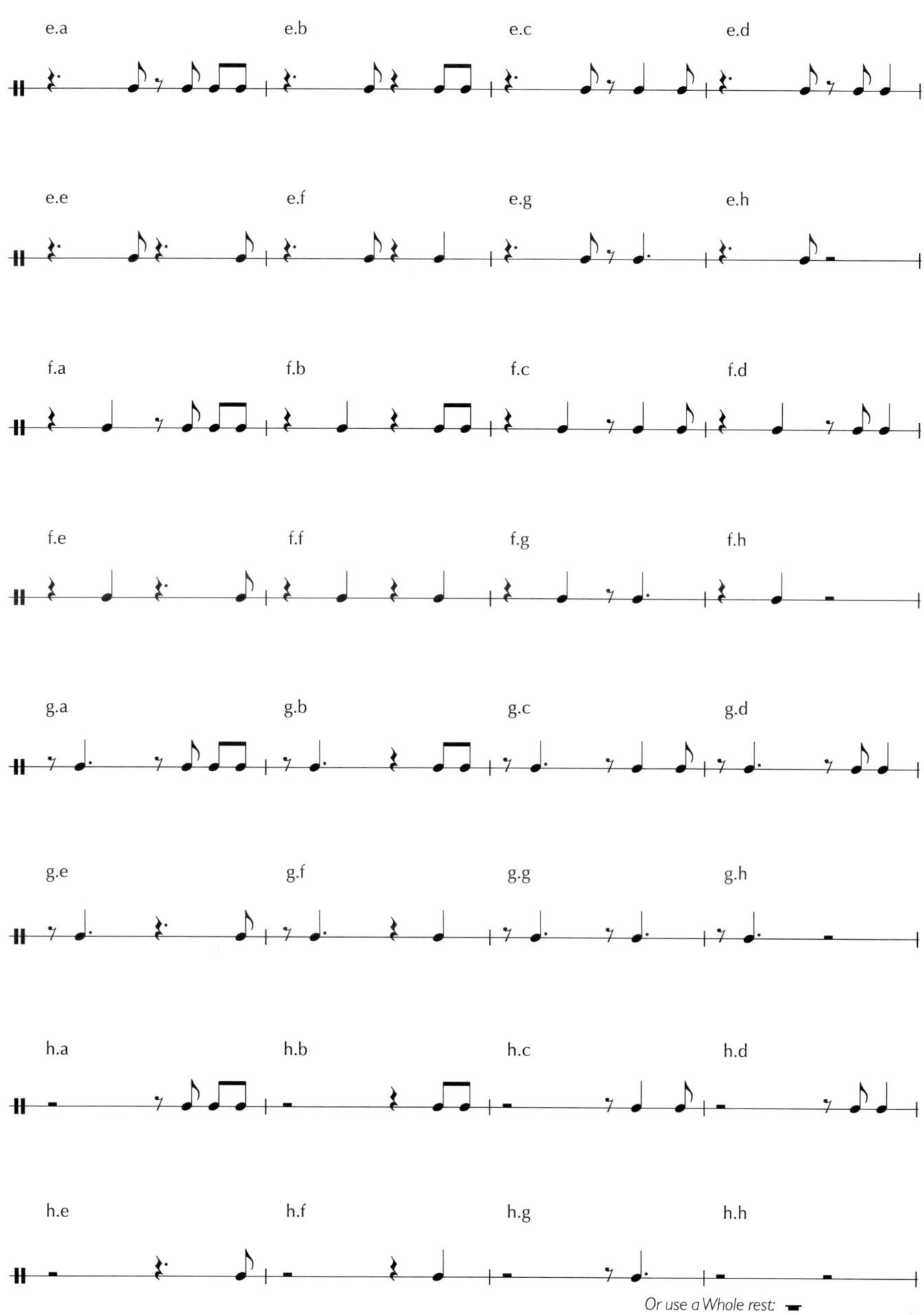

Or use a Whole rest:

Exercise 1g

Same as Exercise 1f but with ties instead of rests.

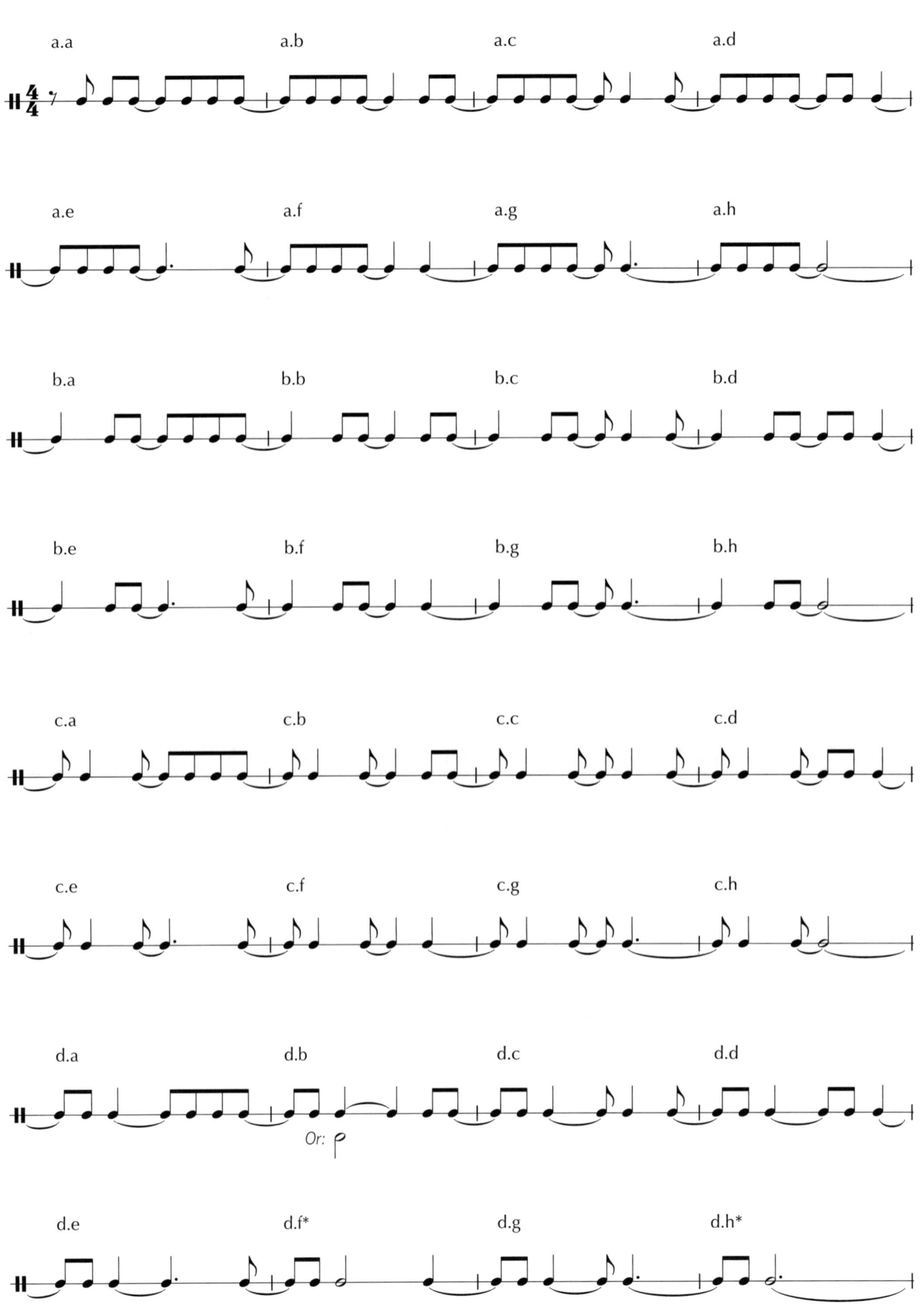

These rhythms are rewritten to a more common note value but the meaning is the same as if they had been written with a tie between the notes in the bar.

Exercise 1g cont.

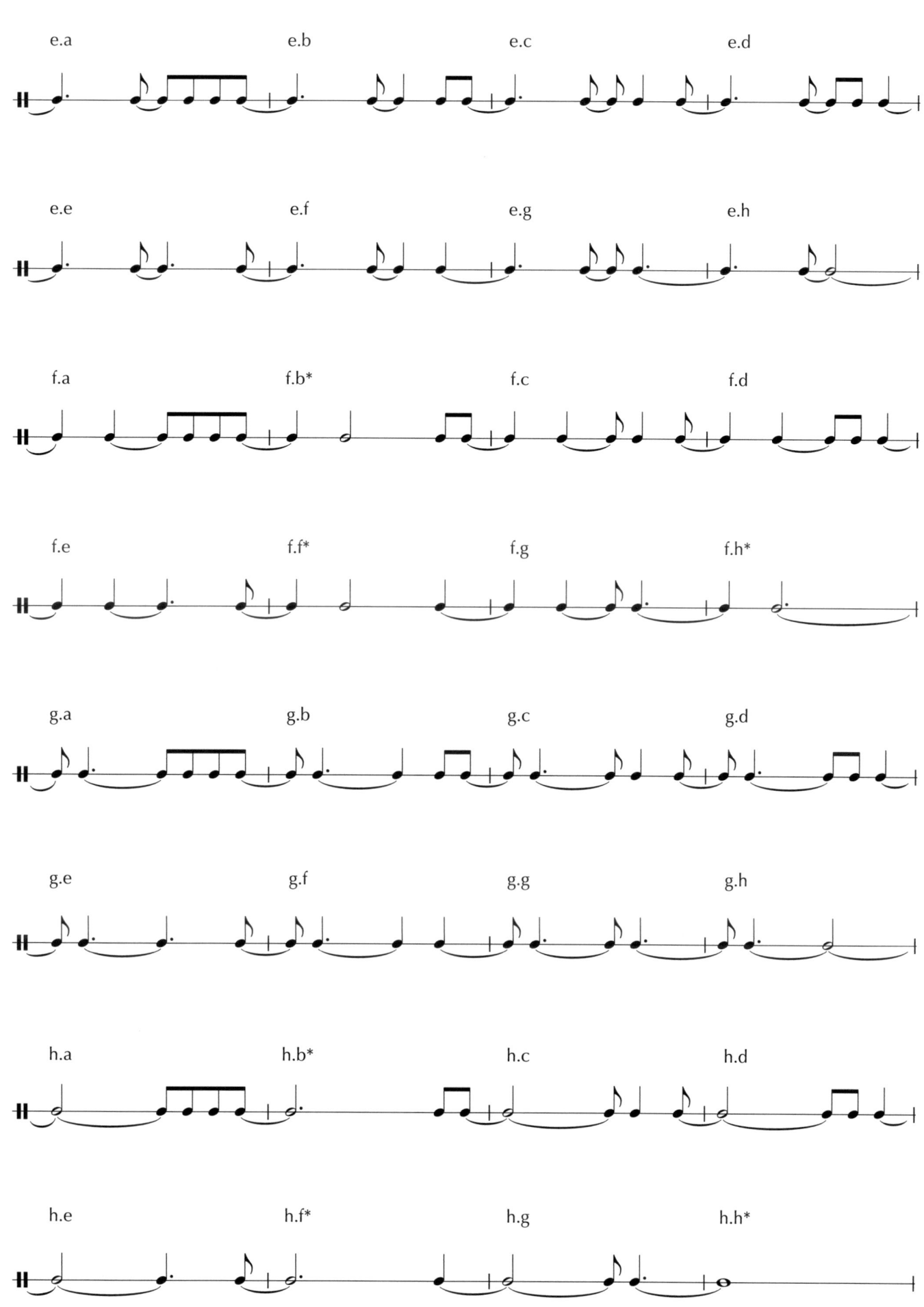

Exercise 1h

Combinations of ties and rests.

Exercise 1h cont.

Exercise 1i

Combinations of ties and rests.

* These rhythms are rewritten to a more common note value, but the meaning is the same as if they had been written with a tie between the notes in the bar.

Exercise 1i cont.

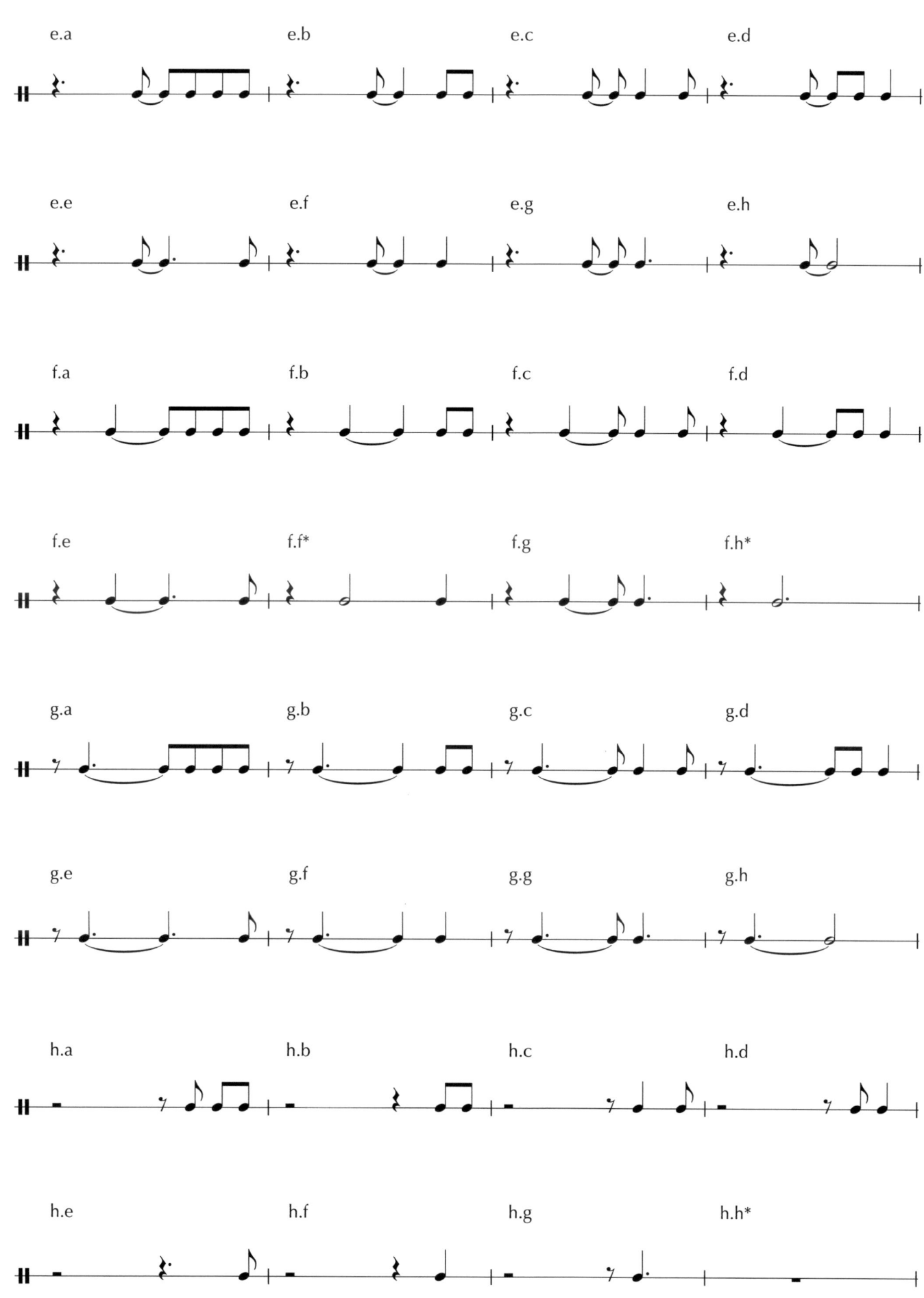

What you have learned

In chapter 1 you have worked with:

- Basic Exercise 1A – eight rhythm-pictures (A-H) created from four eighth notes.

- Basic Exercise 1B – the same rhythms as Basic Exercise 1A but with the first note replaced by a **rest** of the corresponding value.

- **ties**.

- combinations of ties and rests.

Note: This book should not be read from cover to cover since it is organized into subjects instead of a steady progression. (E.g: The end of chapter 1 is harder than the beginning of chapter 2).

Therefore it is to your advantage to follow the study plan at the end of the book.

CHAPTER 2

Sixteenth notes

Sixteenth notes

In chapter 1 we worked with eight rhythm-pictures derived from four eighth notes:

In chapter 2 we are going to work in the same way as in chapter 1, but with rhythm-pictures derived from four sixteenth notes*:

It's the same principle as in chapter 1: you tie together one or more notes from the four sixteenth notes to create eight rhythm-pictures. (See next page).

We will have the same names: A, B, C, D, E, F, G and H, since they are merely a reference point.

Notice that the sixteenth note pictures resemble the ones from chapter 1:

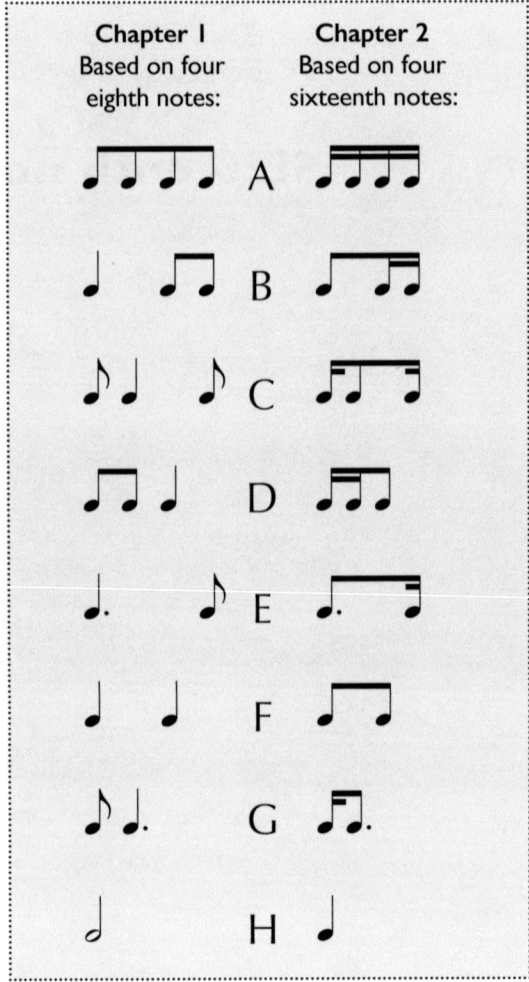

Even if the heading for this chapter is Sixteenth notes, we will be working with other note values. The heading just refers to the four sixteenth notes that the rhythm-pictures are derived from. (See next page).

Eight sixteenth note rhythms

Below, to the right, you see the eight rhythm-pictures that we will work with in this chapter. To the left you see how these pictures have been created using ties, just in the same way as in chapter 1.

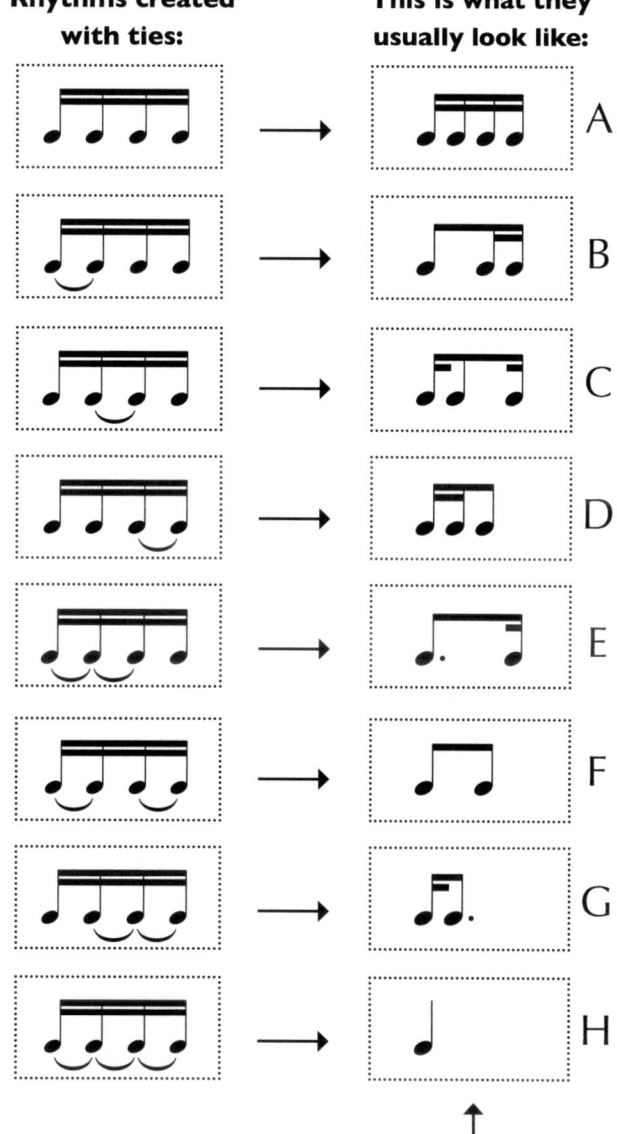

These are the rhythms we will start with in this chapter.

2/4-time

We will practice these eight rhythms in the same way as before, by putting them into bars. But this time we will be using **2/4-time**. (You can read more about time signatures in chapter 11).

The rhythm-pictures in chapter 1 spanned over **two beats** (half a bar in 4/4-time). But in this chapter the rhythm-pictures span over just **one beat** (half a bar in 2/4-time). By using 2/4-time we can put one rhythm on each side of the invisible line in the middle of the bar also in this chapter. Now, go to the next page and practice **Basic Exercise 2A**.

BASIC EXERCISE
2A

IMPORTANT EXERCISE

You can find all Basic Exercises with sound on our website:

www.khmp.se

In this exercise bars are divided by an **invisible line** in the middle, just as in chapter 1. The big difference here is that we are using 2/4-time instead of 4/4-time. We will put **one of the eight rhythms** (A-H) on the left side of the invisible line and a **quarter rest** on the right side:

It looks like this:

1. Start a metronome or a steady beat at **60-65 BPM** (beats per minute).

2. Your teacher sings/plays **rhythm A** below. Student repeats. (While looking at the rhythm). Repeat it until you know it.

3. Go to **rhythm B** and learn in the same way as rhythm A. Listen and repeat. (While looking at the rhythm).

4. Alternate between rhythm A and rhythm B.
   Don't forget the quarter rest at the end of each bar.

5. Add one rhythm at a time until you have mastered all eight rhythms (A-H).

Remember to practice with a steady pulse. (With a metronome or a person playing a steady beat).

Note:
See each rhythm
as a picture!

BERFORE YOU MOVE ON!   *Make sure you know all eight rhythms (A-H) before you move on!*

. . . .

Let's fill a bar with rhythms

On the following pages you will find different combinations of the eight rhythms from **Basic Exercise 2A**.

Above each bar in the exercises there are two letters, for example A.D.
These letters tell you which rhythms are in that bar. The first letter points to the first half of the bar and the second letter points to the second half.
Just as in chapter 1:

These letters are there to help you, or your teacher, to identify combinations that you are struggling with, or handle with ease, for that matter. They are also a guide for you to communicate with. Like:
Teacher: – Let's take it from D.E. (The letters are instead of bar numbers).

It is important that you see each bar as two parts (two halves) or as two pictures, to begin with!

Remember to practice with a steady pulse.
(E.g. With a metronome or a person playing a steady beat).

> **Pro tip!**
> *When playing/singing the first half of a bar you must try to look ahead to the second half of the bar at the same time. This will force your eyes to move forward and be prepared for what is ahead. When playing the second half of the bar your eyes should already be on the first half of the next bar, and so on.*
>
> *This is hard in the beginning but after a while you will master it. Start with half a bar and perhaps you can manage a whole bar or more in the future.*

Remember to divide each bar into two parts and see each rhythm as a picture.

Exercise 2a

Rhythms from Basic Exercise 2A.

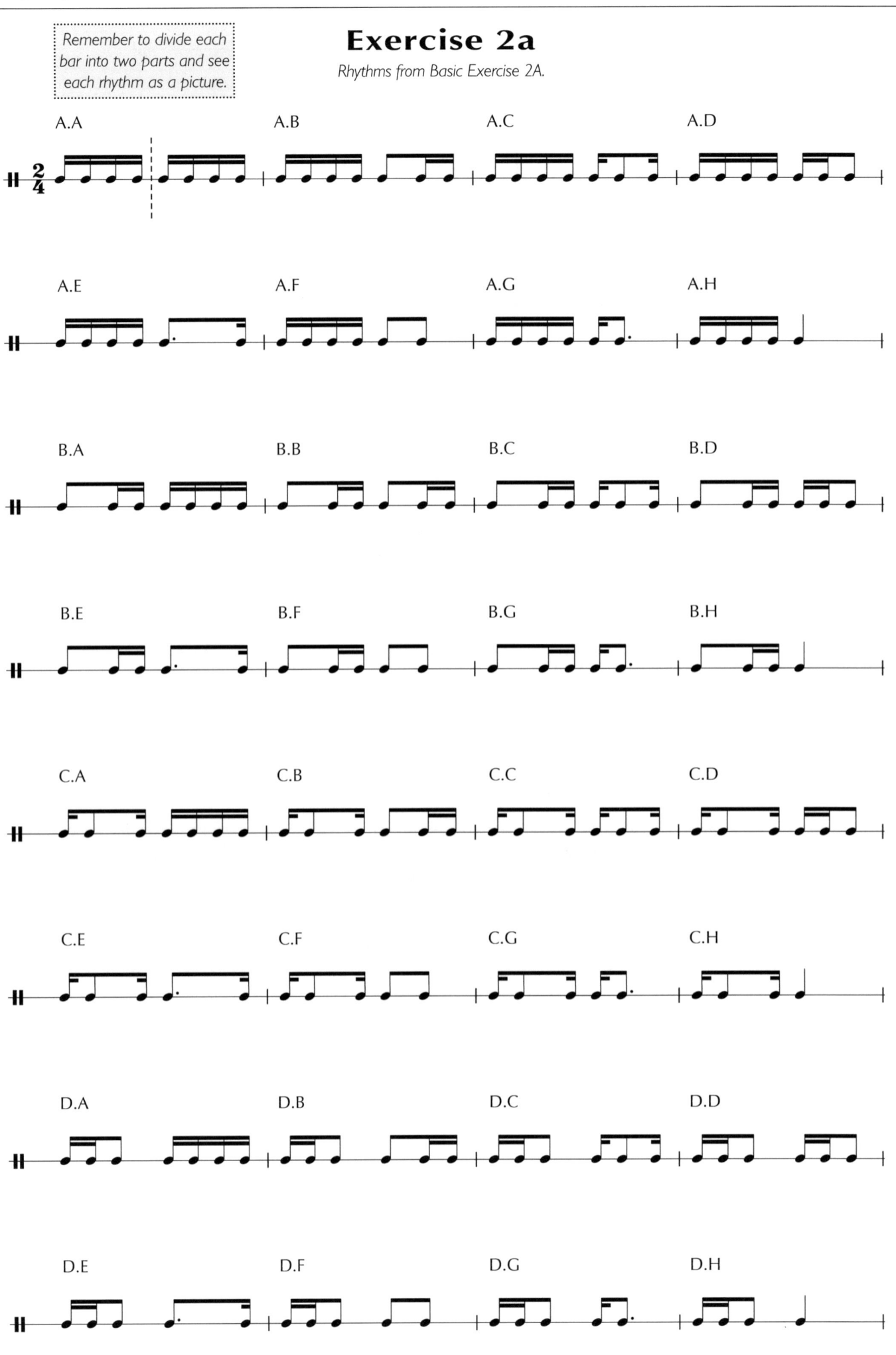

Exercise 2a cont.

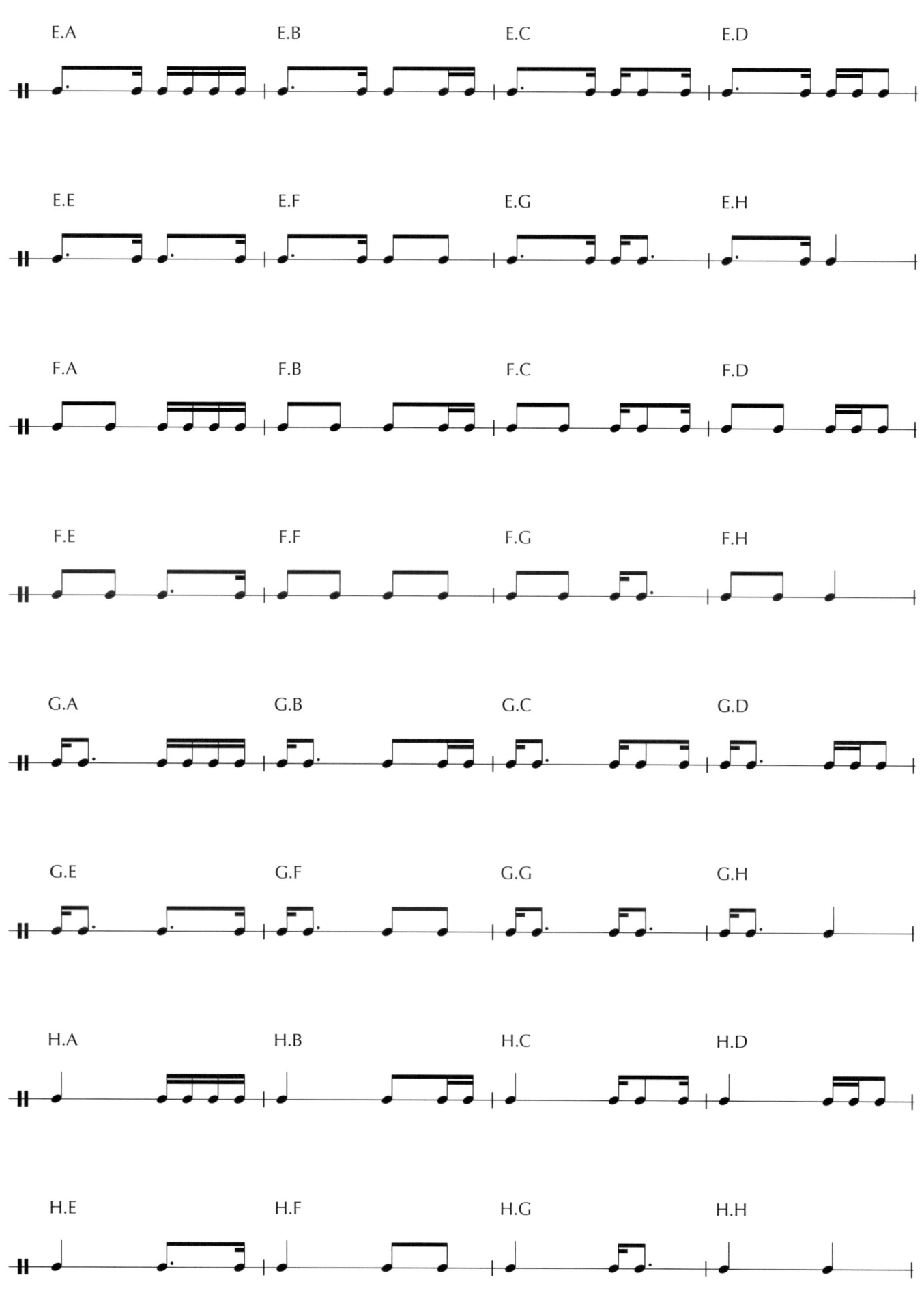

BEFORE YOU MOVE ON!

Before you move on in this chapter, which will develop the eight rhythms you have learned with rests and ties, I suggest that you jump to chapter 3. There you will combine rhythms from chapter 1 and chapter 2. In addition to that you will also work in 3/4-time. **Remember to follow the study plan at the end of the book for a natural progression.**

Rests in chapter 2 (See also the Appendix)

In chapter 1, I told you that rests are **active**.

I also said that you should see rests as **silent notes** or **played silence**. You should also look at rests **in a bigger context** and see them together with the notes that come after.

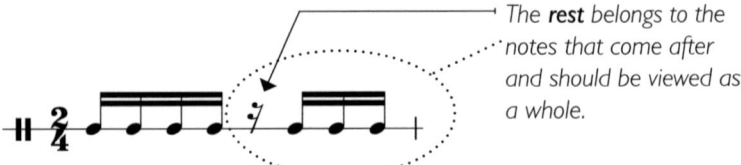

*The **rest** belongs to the notes that come after and should be viewed as a whole.*

In a moment we will jump to **Basic Exercise 2B** where you will practice eight new rhythm-pictures, built on Basic Exercise 2A, with the only difference that the first note in each rhythm is replaced by a **rest** of the corresponding value.

They are rehearsed in the same way as in earlier Basic Exercises where your teacher plays the rhythms and you mimic them, while looking at the rhythm-pictures. It is the same method as learning a new language.

BASIC EXERCISE

2B

RESTS

IMPORTANT EXERCISE

You can find all Basic Exercises with sound on our website:

www.khmp.se

1. Start a metronome or a steady beat at **60-65 BPM** (beats per minute).

2. Your teacher sings/plays **rhythm A** below. Student repeats. (While looking at the rhythm). Repeat it until you know it.

3. Go to **rhythm B** and learn it in the same way as rhythm A. Listen and repeat. (While looking at the rhythm).

4. Alternate between rhythm A and B.
   Don't forget the quarter rest at the end of each bar.

5. Add one rhythm at a time until you have mastered all eight rhythms (A-H).

6. Remember to practice with a steady pulse. (with a metronome or a person playing a steady beat).

7. Don't move on to Exercise 2b on page 46 until you are comfortable with the rhythms below.

Note:
See each rhythm as a picture!

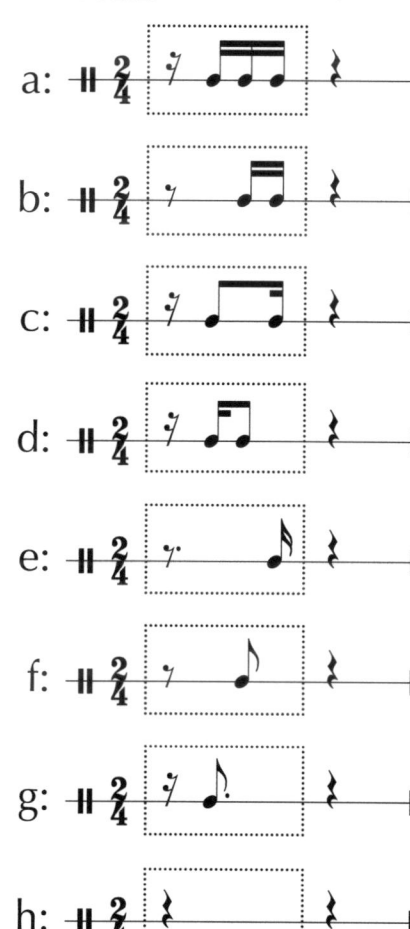

*Small letters above the bars in the exercises ahead, mean that the rhythm-pictures are modified with a rest (or a tie), while **capital letters** points to the original rhythm-pictures.*

Remember to divide each bar into two parts and see each rhythm as a picture.

Exercise 2b

Rhythms from Basic Exercises 2A and 2B.

Exercise 2b cont.

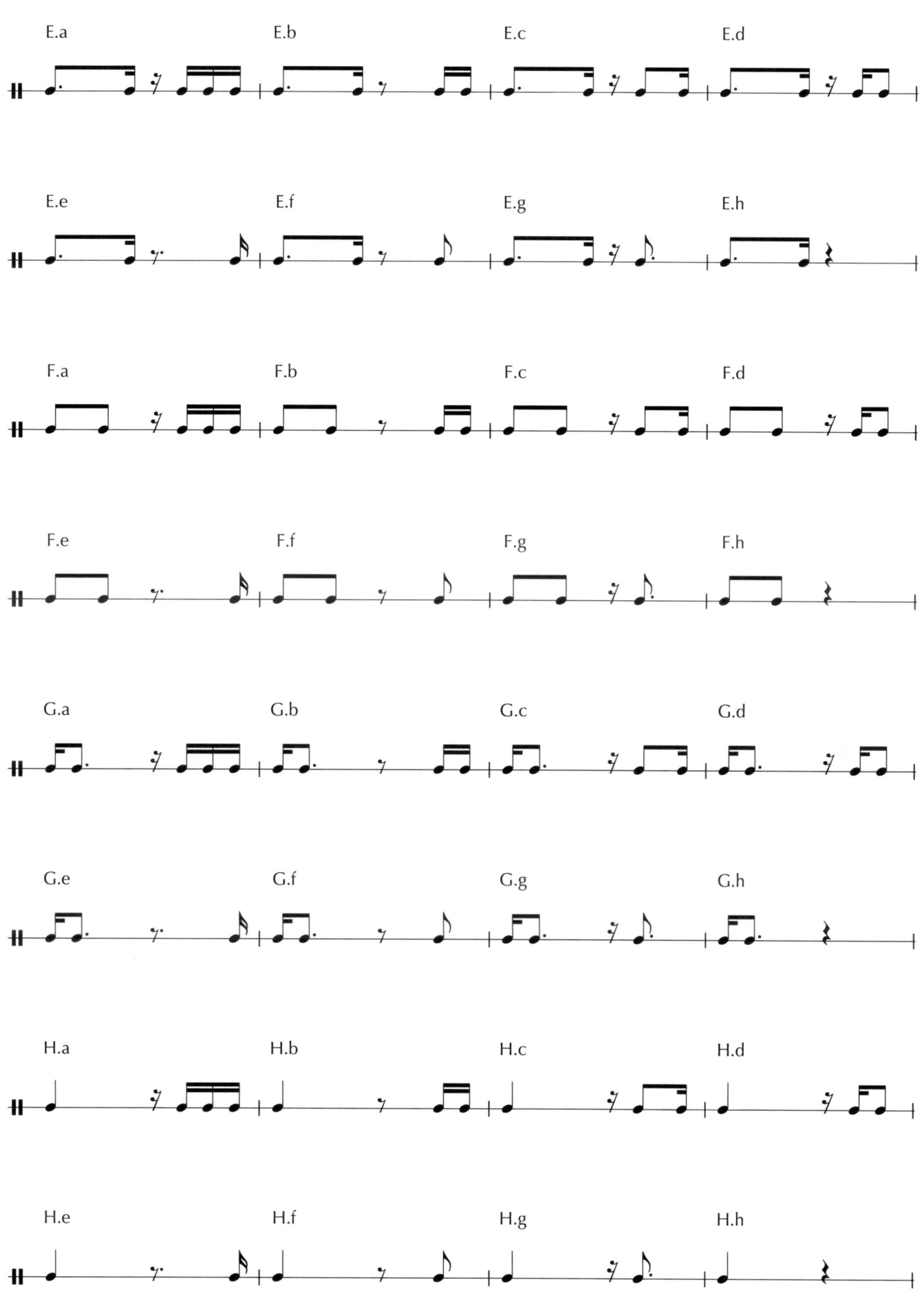

Information about ties is found in chapter 1, page 20-21.

Exercise 2c

Same as Exercise 2b but with ties instead of rests.

A.a   A.b   A.c   A.d

A.e   A.f   A.g   A.h

B.a   B.b   B.c   B.d

B.e   B.f   B.g   B.h

C.a   C.b   C.c   C.d

C.e   C.f   C.g   C.h

D.a   D.b   D.c   D.d

D.e   D.f   D.g   D.h

Exercise 2c cont.

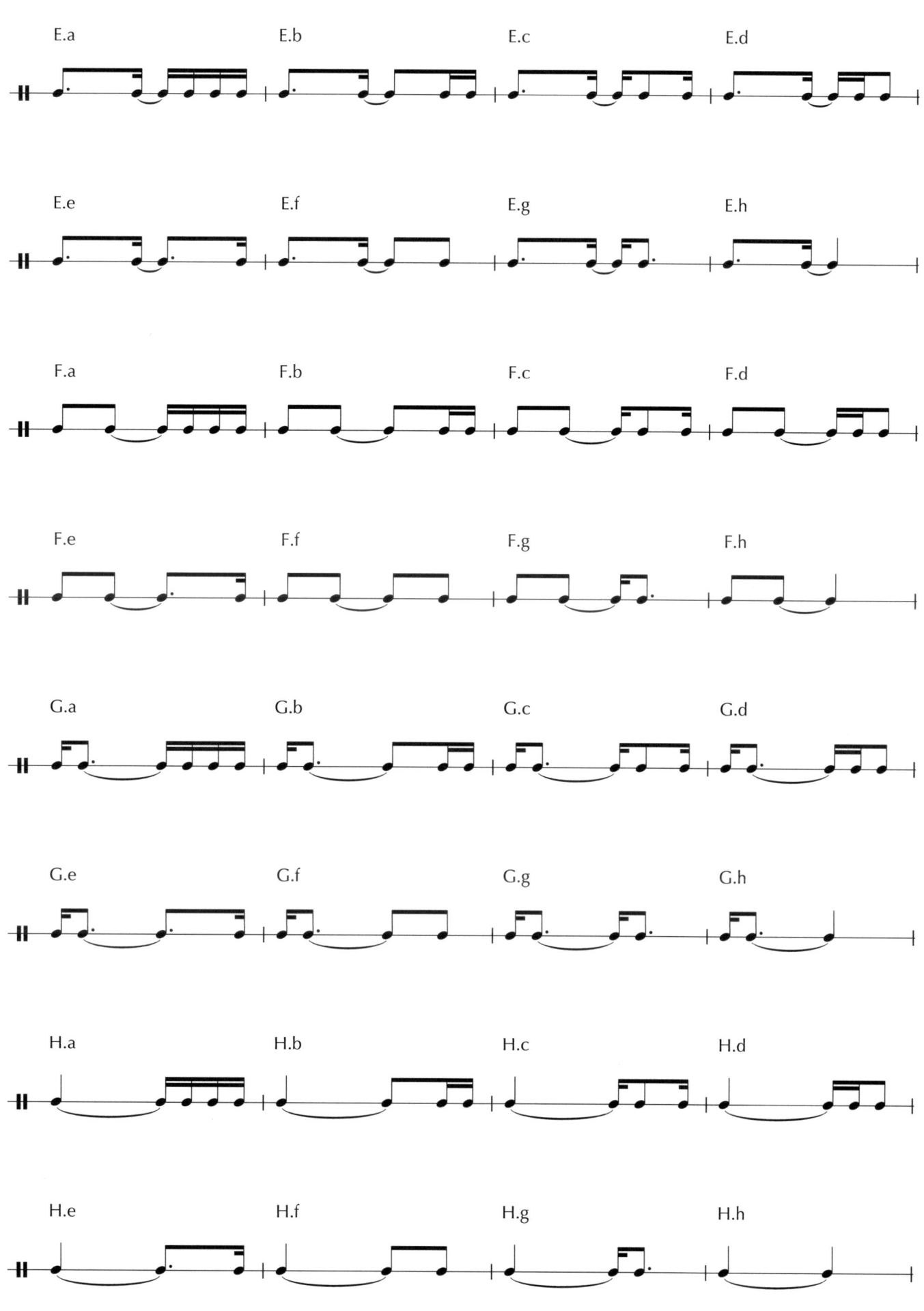

Exercise 2d

Rhythms from Basic Exercises 2B and 2A.

Exercise 2d cont.

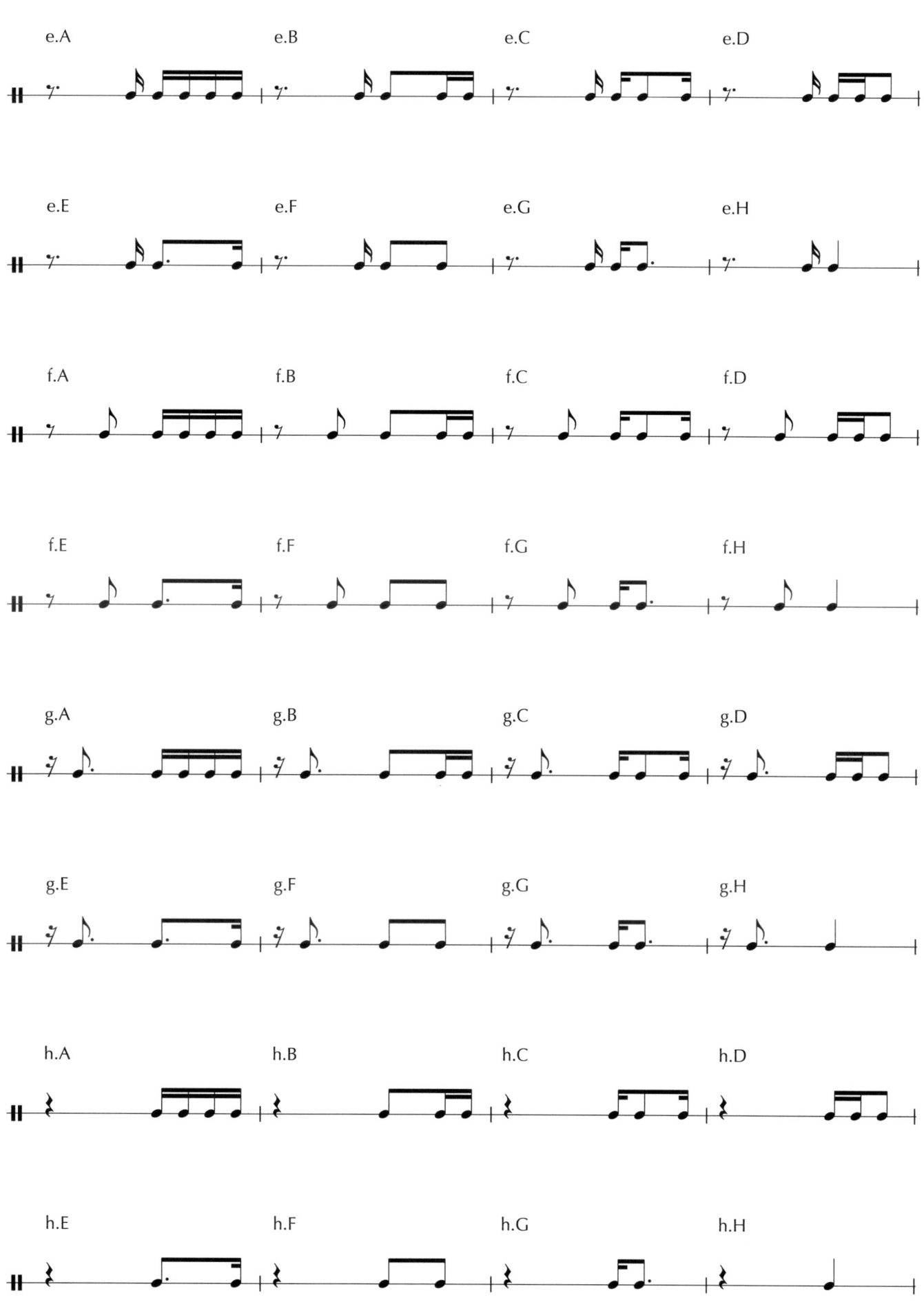

Exercise 2e

Same as Exercise 2d but with ties instead of rests..

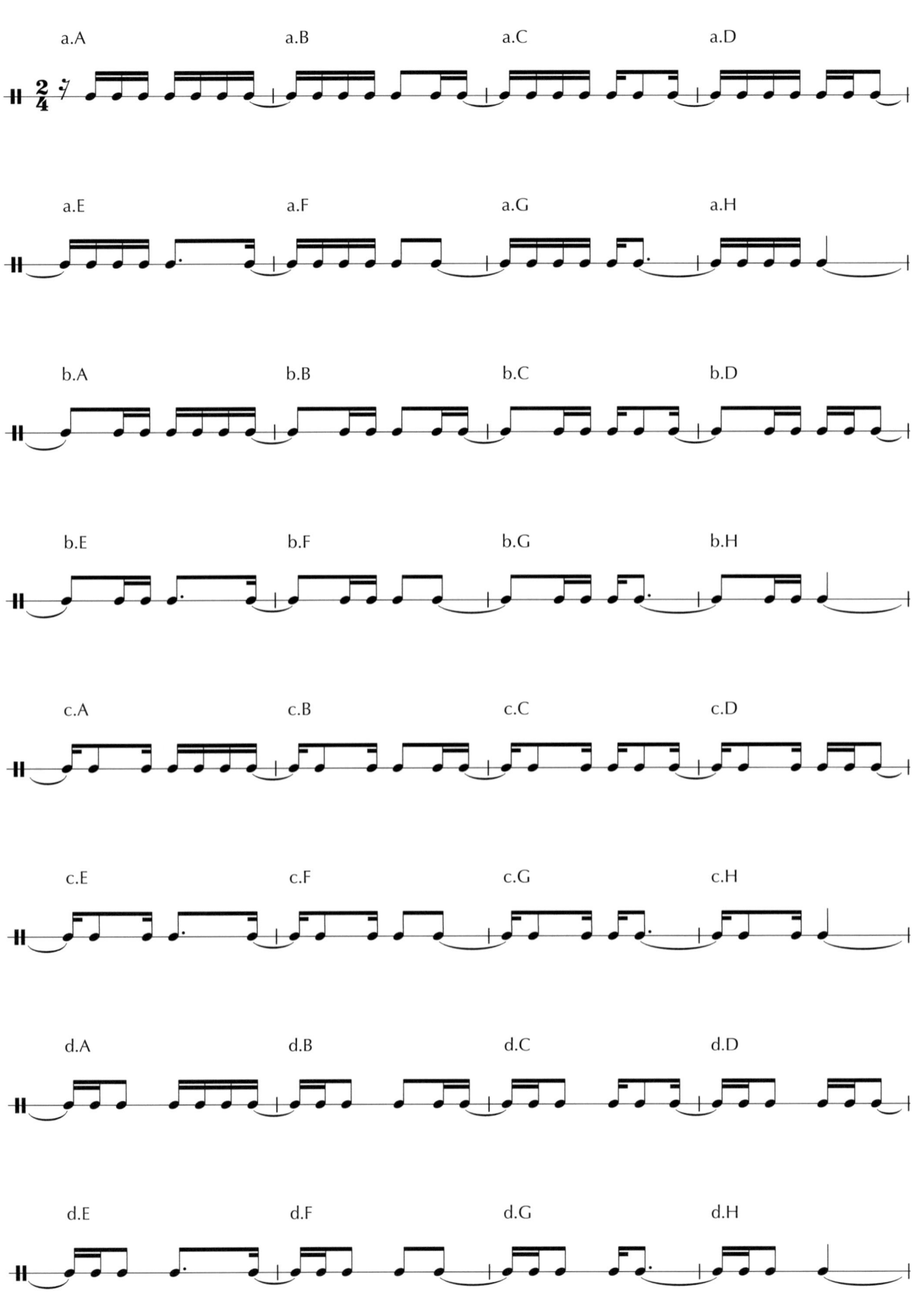

Exercise 2e cont.

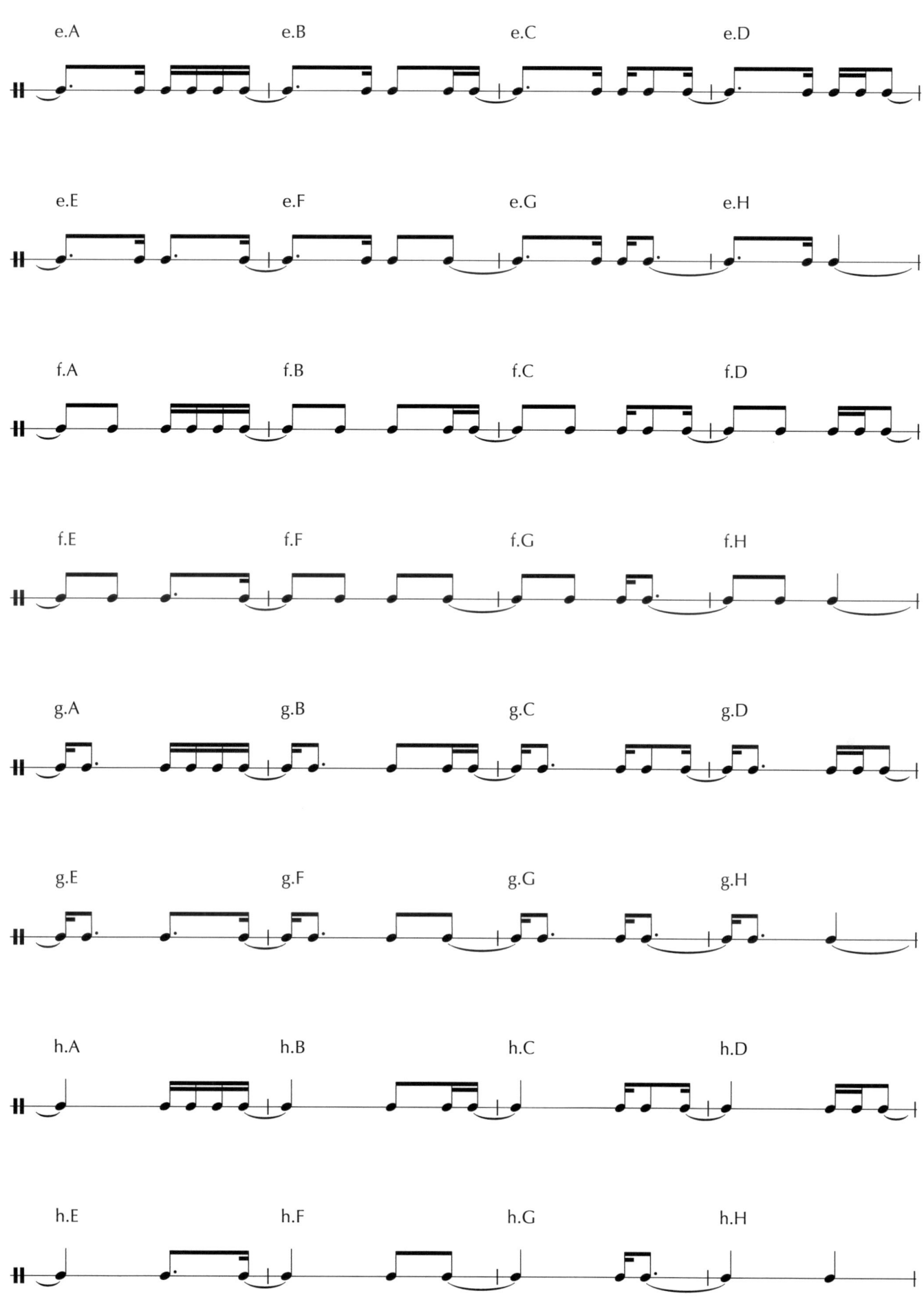

Exercise 2f

Rhythms from Basic Exercise 2B.

Exercise 2f cont.

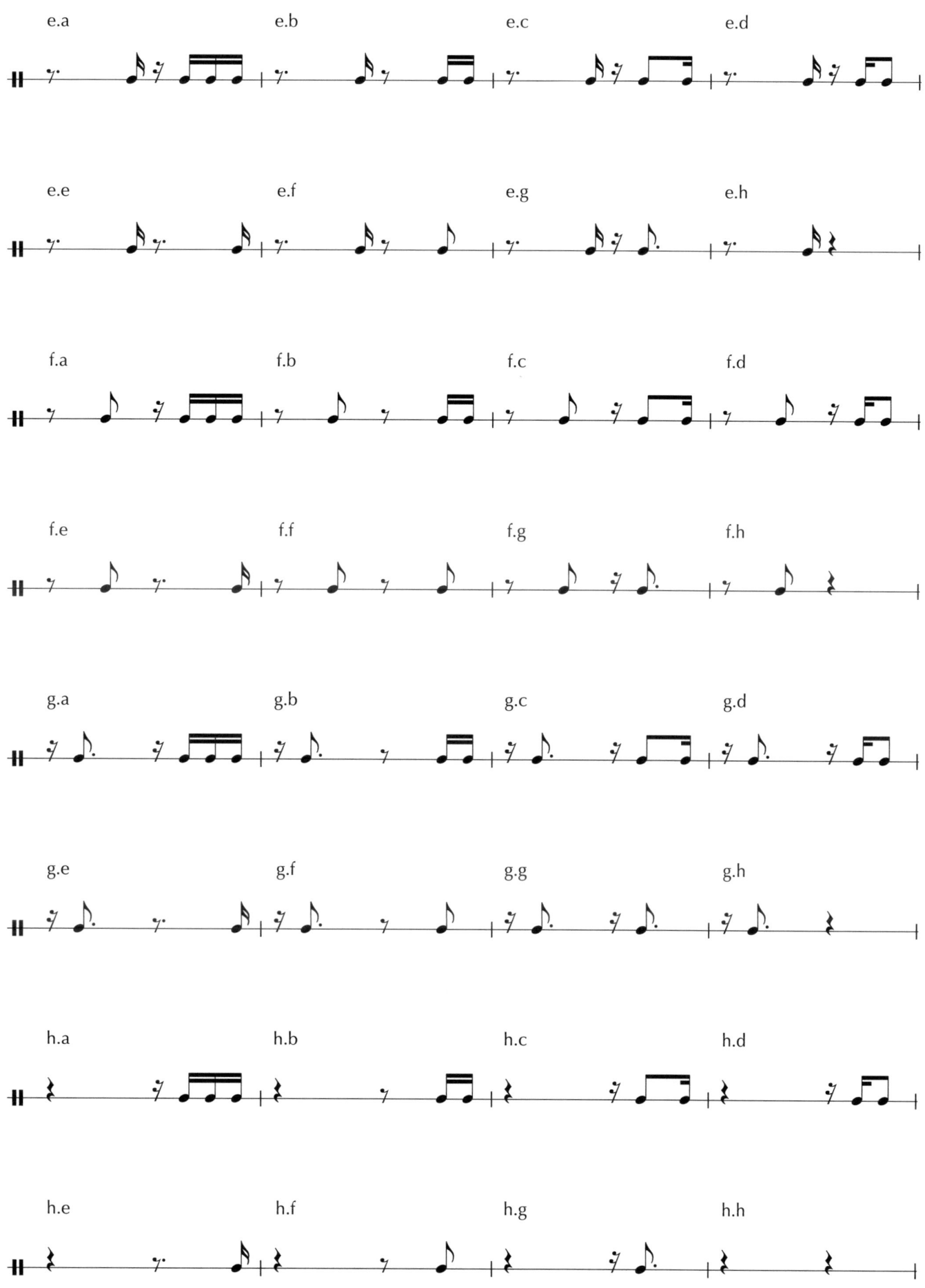

Exercise 2g

Same as Exercise 2f but with ties instead of rests.

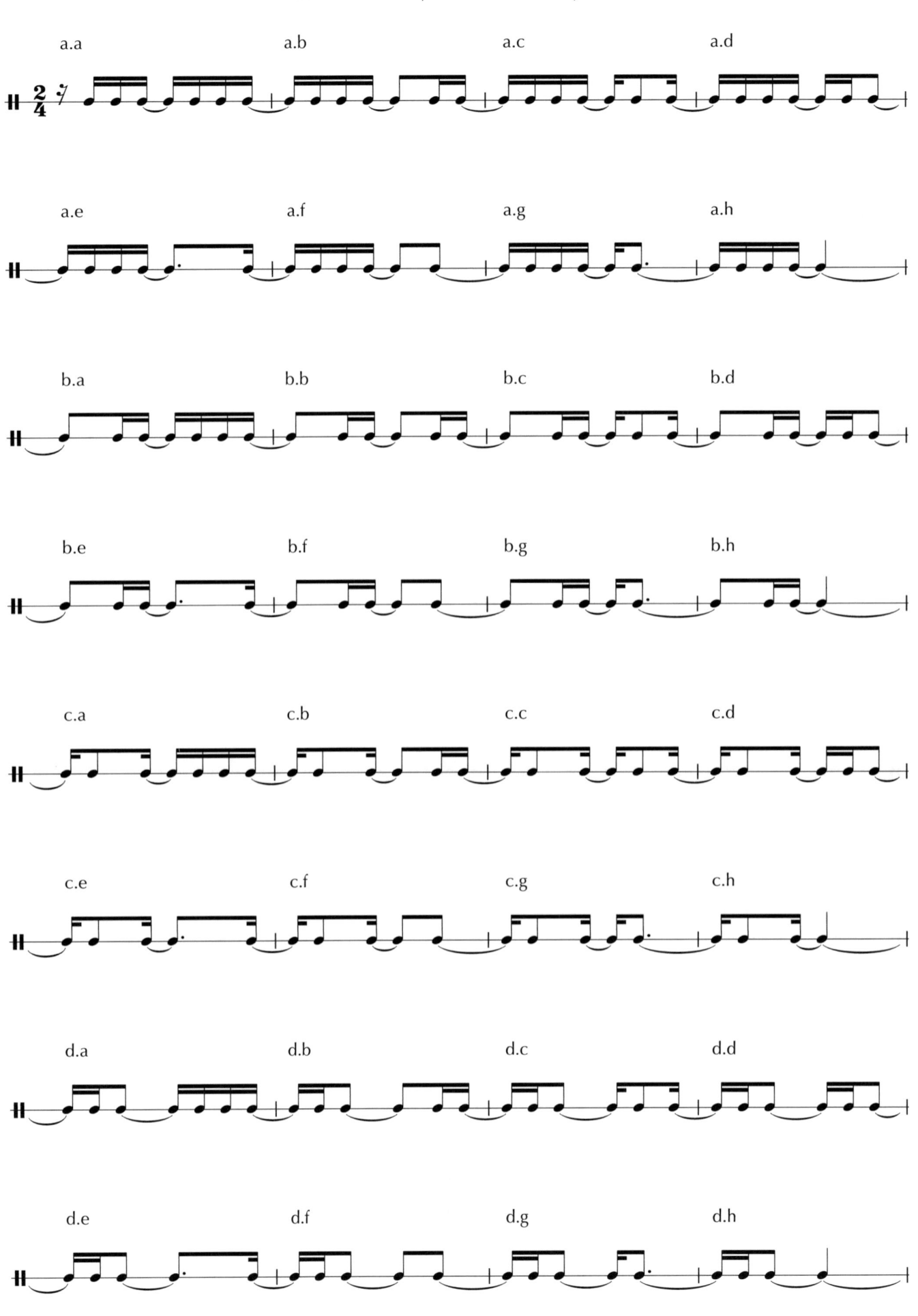

Exercise 2g cont.

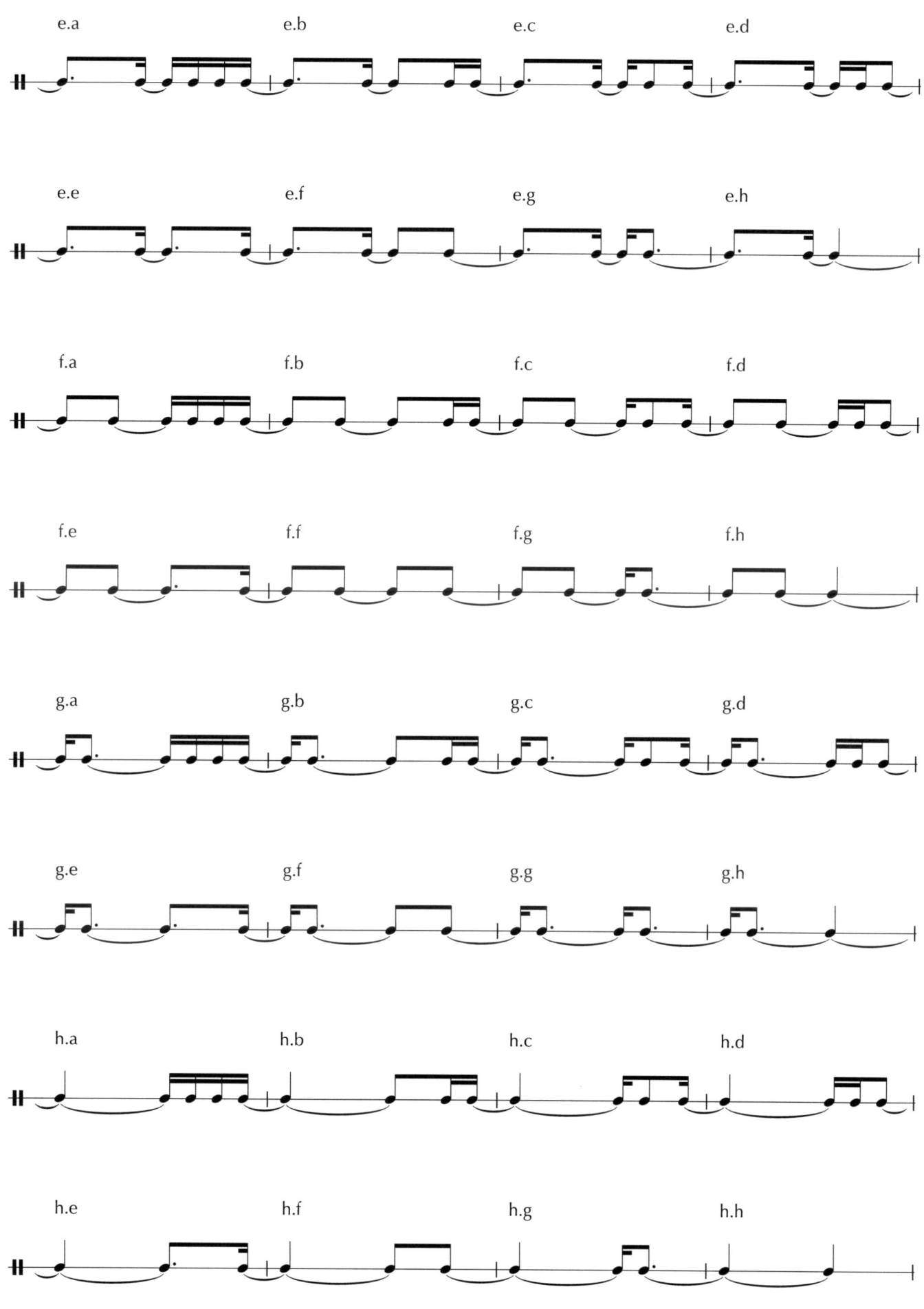

Exercise 2h

Combinations of rests and ties.

Exercise 2h cont.

Exercise 2i

Combinations of rests and ties.

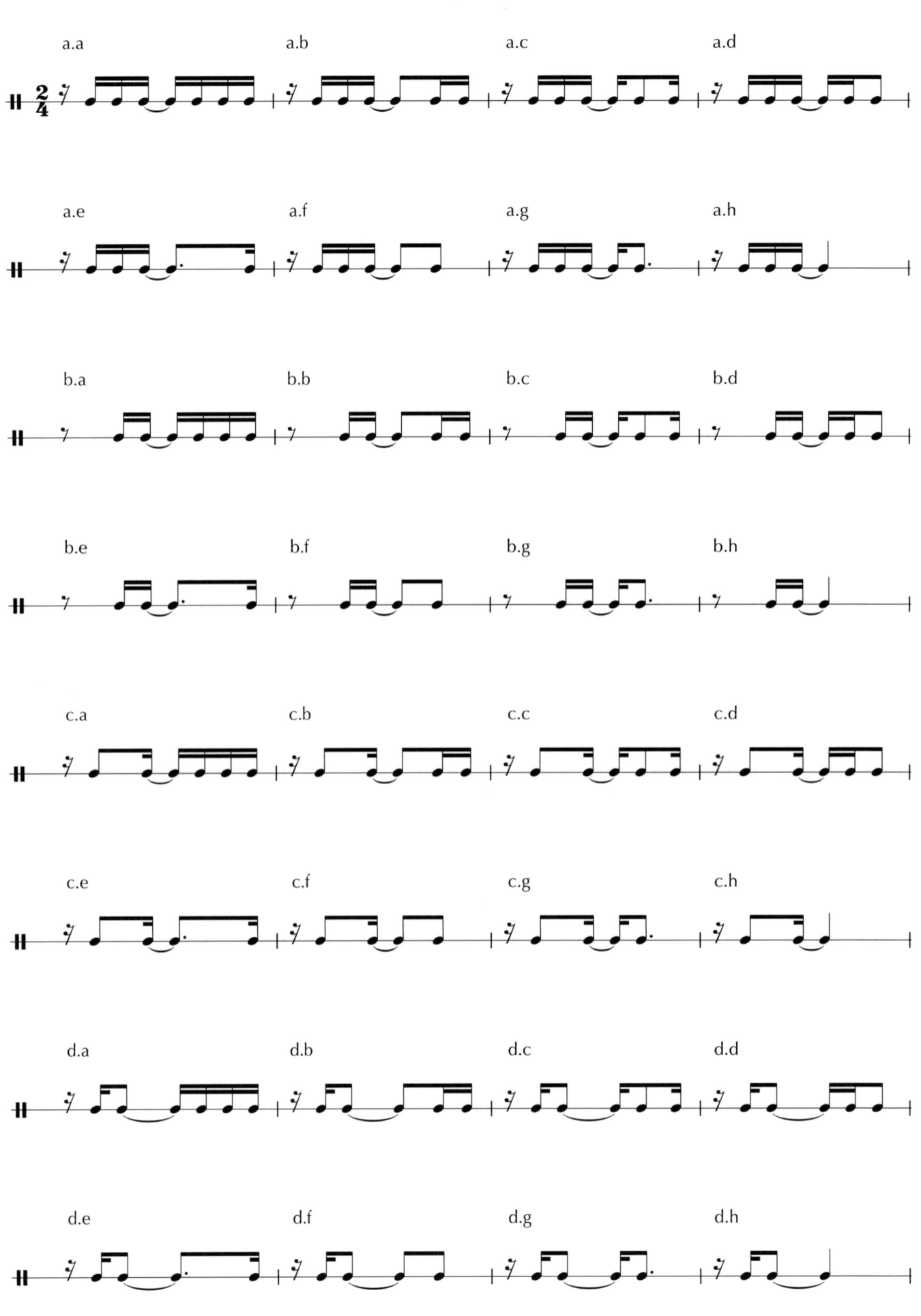

Exercise 2i cont.

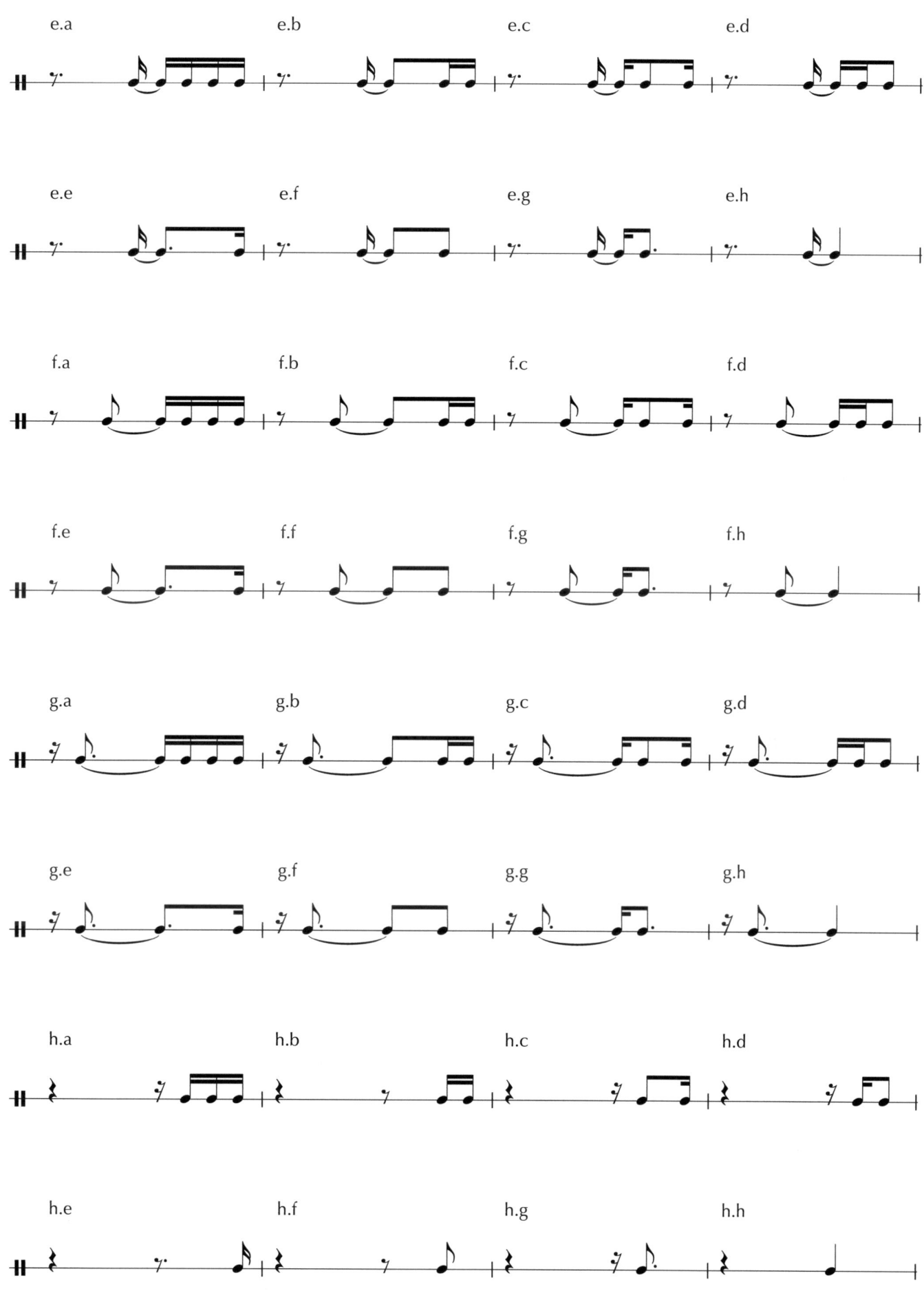

What you have learned in chapter 2

In this chapter you have worked with:

- Basic Exercise 2A – eight rhythm-pictures (A-H) created from four sixteenth notes.

- Basic Exercise 2B – the same rhythms as Basic Exercise 2A but with the first note replaced by a **rest** of the corresponding value.

- Exercises 2a-2i, containing combinations of rhythms from Basic Exercise 2A and Basic Exercise 2B plus ties between rhythms within the bars and ties between the bars. You have also worked with combinations of ties and rests.

Note: This book should not be read from cover to cover since it is organized into subjects instead of a steady progression. (E.g: The end of chapter 1 is harder than the beginning of chapter 2).

Therefore it is to your advantage to follow the study plan at the end of the book.

CHAPTER 3

**Combinations from
chapter 1 and chapter 2**
(3/4-time)

Combinations from chapter 1 and chapter 2 (3/4-time)

In this chapter we are going to combine rhythms from chapter 1 and chapter 2. Since the rhythms in chapter 1 spanned over two beats and the rhythms in chapter 2 spanned over one beat we can conveniently combine them into 3/4-time. (2+1=3). *You can read more about time signatures in chapter 11.*

3/4-time

With 3/4-time it is not possible to split a bar in two while keeping an equal amount of beats on each side of the invisible line in the middle of the bar.

Instead, we can divide the bar in three different ways:

1).   1 + 2 beats:

2).   2 + 1 beats:

3).   1 + 1 + 1 beats:

A new rest

We will soon do exercises according to the three ways mentioned above. In these exercises we will see an alternative way of looking at a **dotted quarter rest**, found in **rhythm e** in Basic Exercise 1B. on page 17.

So far we have used this rest: Now we will also use this variation:

   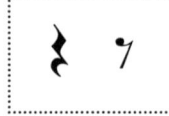

Both ways are common so you must be familiar with both of them.

Variation no. 1 (1 + 2 beats)

In the first exercises that follows we'll be using rhythms from chapter 2 on beat one in the bar, and rhythms from chapter 1 on beat two and three. The letter combination above each bar points to the rhythm used from each chapter respectively.

Like this:

From chapter 2   From chapter 1

Start a metronome or a steady beat at 60-100 BPM (beats per minute) and play Exercise 3-1(a) that begins on the next page. ⟶

. . . .

Make your own exercises

To save some space in this book I have decided to let you make your own exercises.

Take photo copies of Exercise 3-1(a) on the next page and write **ties** on the copies as follows:

1. Write ties between the rhythm-pictures within the bar. (Var. C):

2. Write ties between the bars. (Var. E):

3. Write ties between both the rhythm-pictures within the bar AND between the bars. (Var. G):

Make a mark on the copy which variation you have choosen: C, E or G.

Note: Exercises 3-2 (B, D and F) don't have ties but rests, so they are still in the book.

Exercise 3-1:

A - No TIES (original)
☐ C - Ties between the rhythm-pictures within the bar
☐ E - Ties between the bars
☐ G - Ties according to both C and E

Exercise 3-1 cont.

A - No TIES (original)

☐ **C** - *Ties between the rhythm-pictures within the bar*

☐ **E** - *Ties between the bars*

☐ **G** - *Ties according to both C and E*

MAKE COPIES OF THIS PAGE!
Write TIES according to: C, E or G.

Exercise 3-1b

Rhythms from Basic Exercise 2a and 1b.

Exercise 3-1b cont.

Exercise 3-1d

Rhythms from Basic Exercise 2b and 1a.

Exercise 3-1d cont.

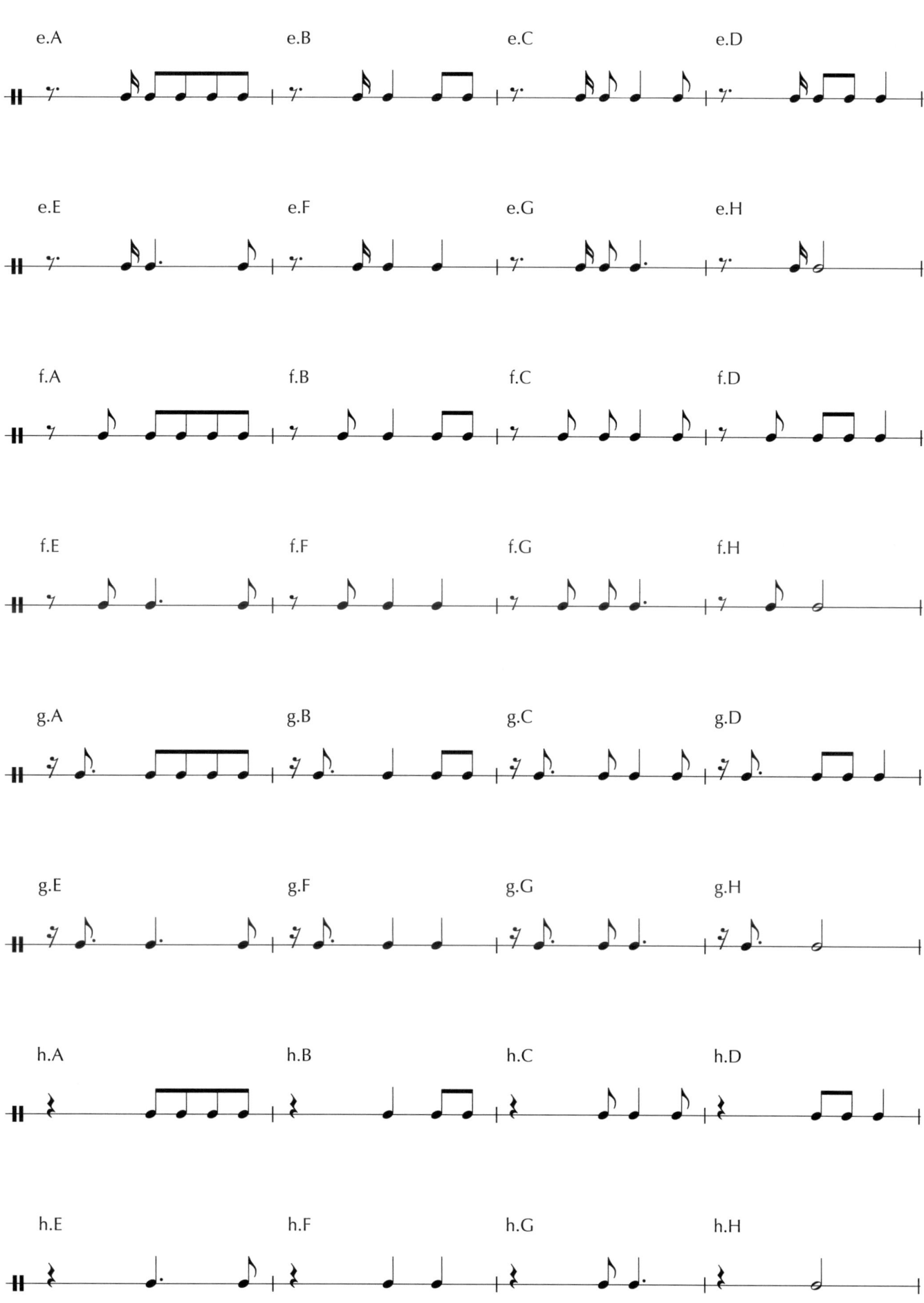

Exercise 3-1f

Rhythms from Basic Exercise 2b and 1b.

Exercise 3-1f cont.

Or use a **Whole rest**: ▬
This rest indicates silence for a full
bar, no matter what time signature it is.

73

Variation no. 2 (2 + 1 beats)

Let's flip everything and put the rhythms from chapter 1 first. By doing this you will have a more intense training of the rhythms from chapter 2, sixteenth notes.

The letter combination above each bar points to the rhythm used from each chapter respectively.

Like this:

Start a metronome or a steady beat at 60-100 BPM (beats per minute) and play Exercise 3-2(a) that begins on page 76.

Make your own exercises

To save some space in this book I have decided to let you make your own exercises.

Take photo copies of Exercise 3-2(a) on the next page and write **ties** on the copies as follows:

1. Write ties between the rhythm-pictures within the bar. (Var. C):

2. Write ties between the bars. (Var. E):

3. Write ties between both the rhythm-pictures within the bar AND between the bars. (Var. G):

Make a mark on the copy which variation you have choosen: C, E or G.

Note: Exercises 3-2 (B, D and F) don't have ties but rests, so they are still in the book.

Exercise 3-2

A - No TIES (original)
☐ *C - Ties between the rhythm-pictures within the bar*
☐ *E - Ties between the bars*
☐ *G - Ties according to both C and E*

www.khmp.se

Exercise 3-2 cont.

A - No TIES (original)

☐ **C** - *Ties between the rhythm-pictures within the bar*
☐ **E** - *Ties between the bars*
☐ **G** - *Ties according to both C and E*

Exercise 3-2b

Rhythms from Basic Exercise 1a and 2b.

Exercise 3-2b cont.

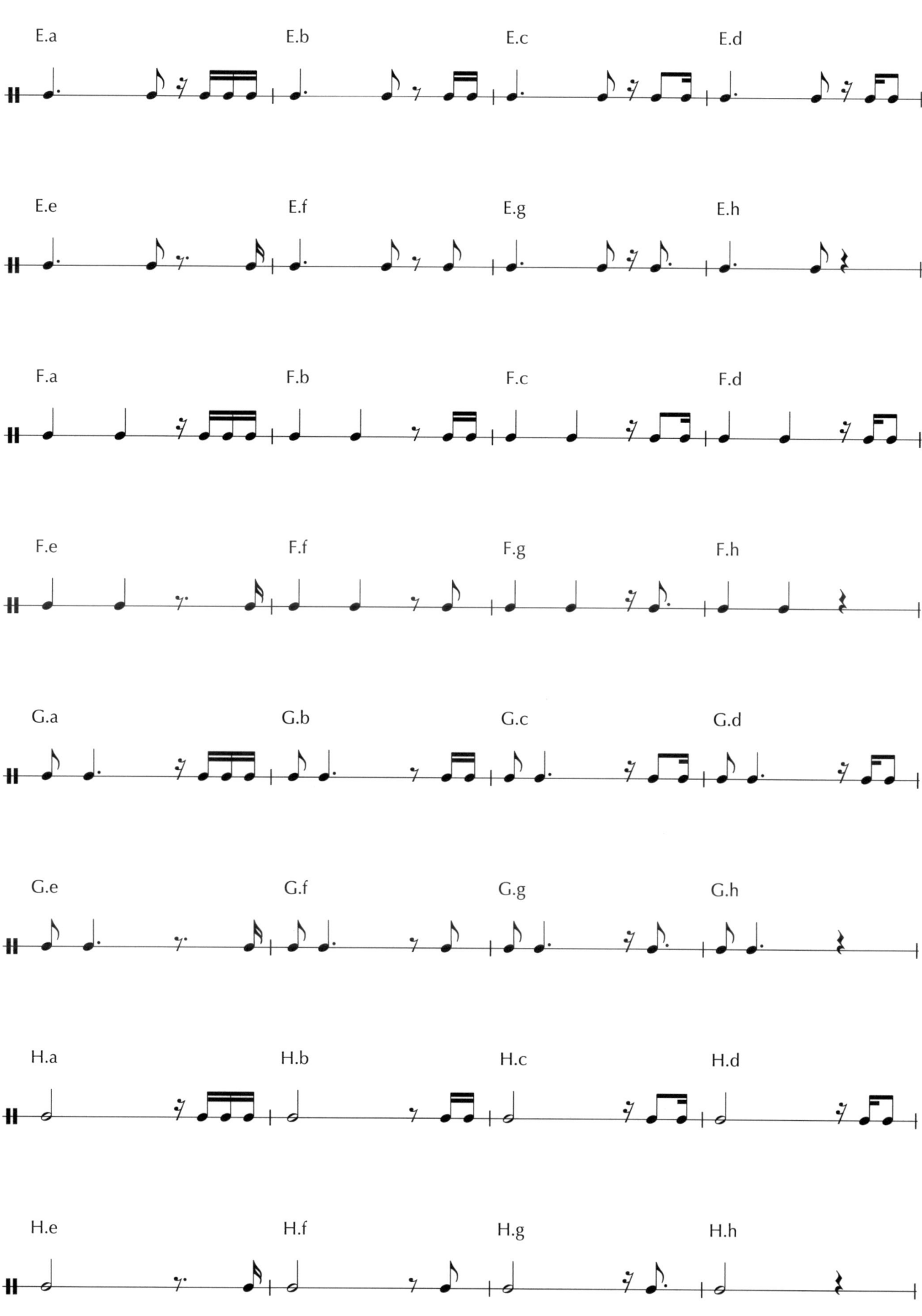

Exercise 3-2d

Rhythms from Basic Exercise 1b and 2a..

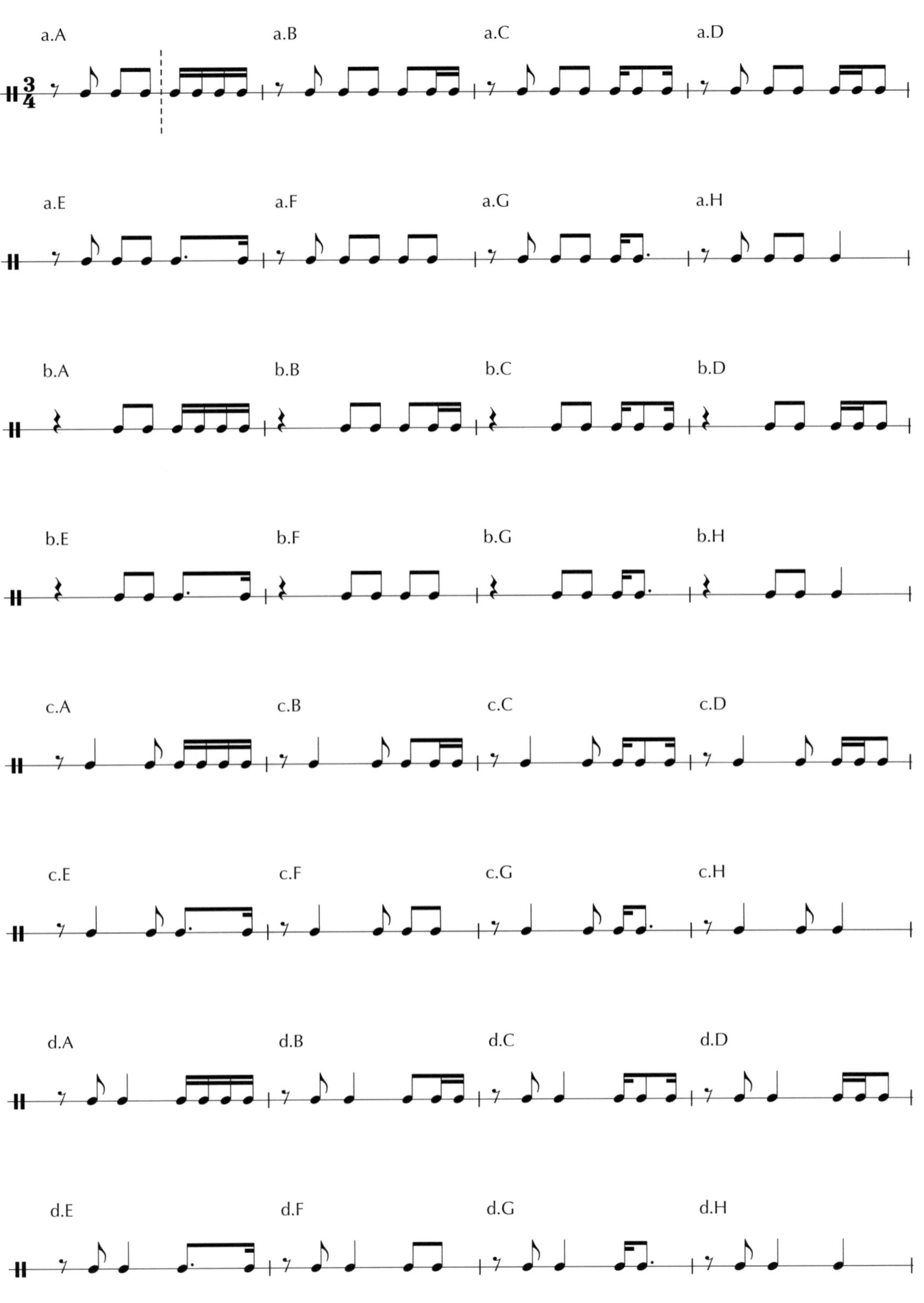

Exercise 3-2d cont.

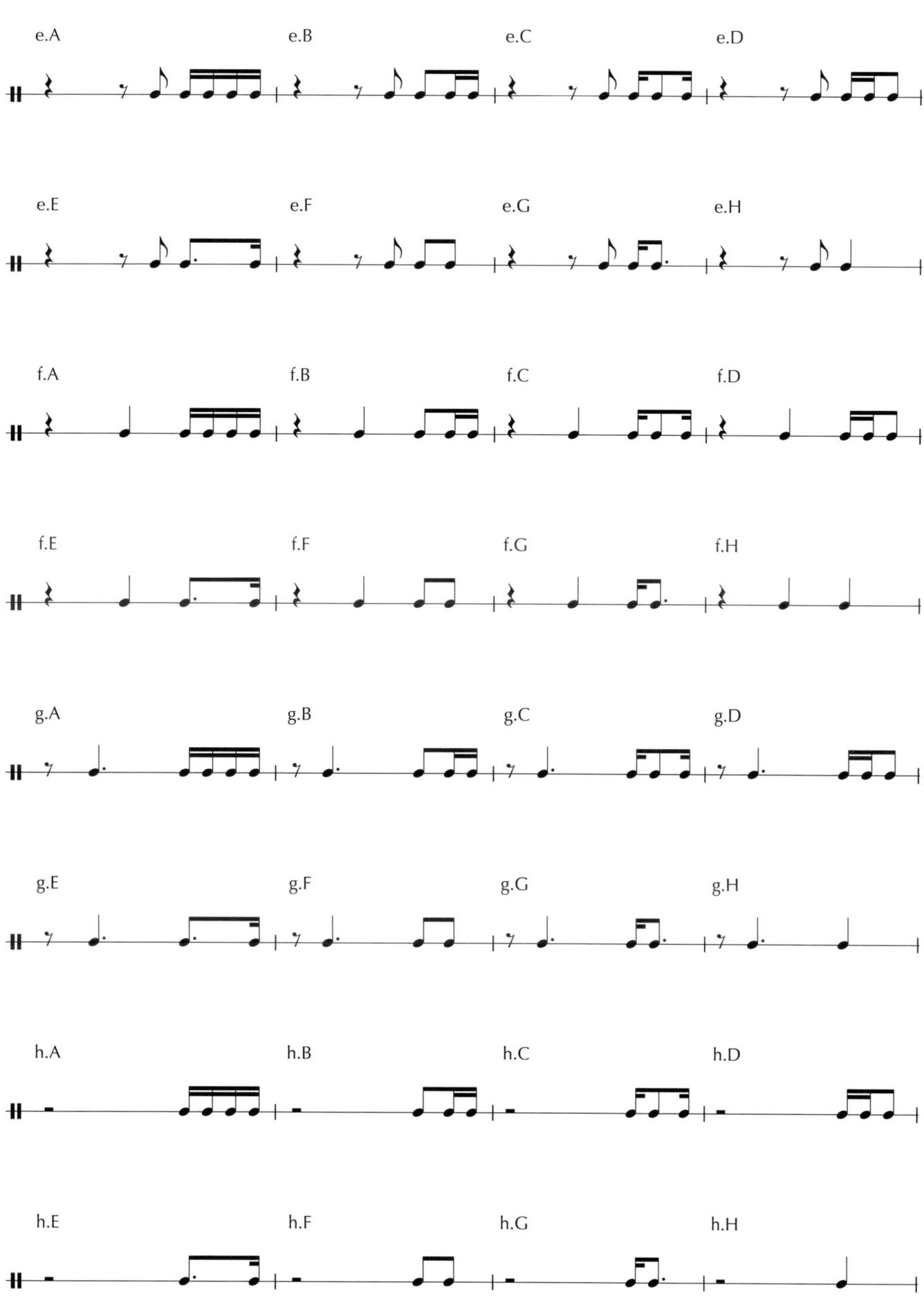

Exercise 3-2f

Rhythms from Basic Exercise 1b and 2b.

Exercise 3-2f cont.

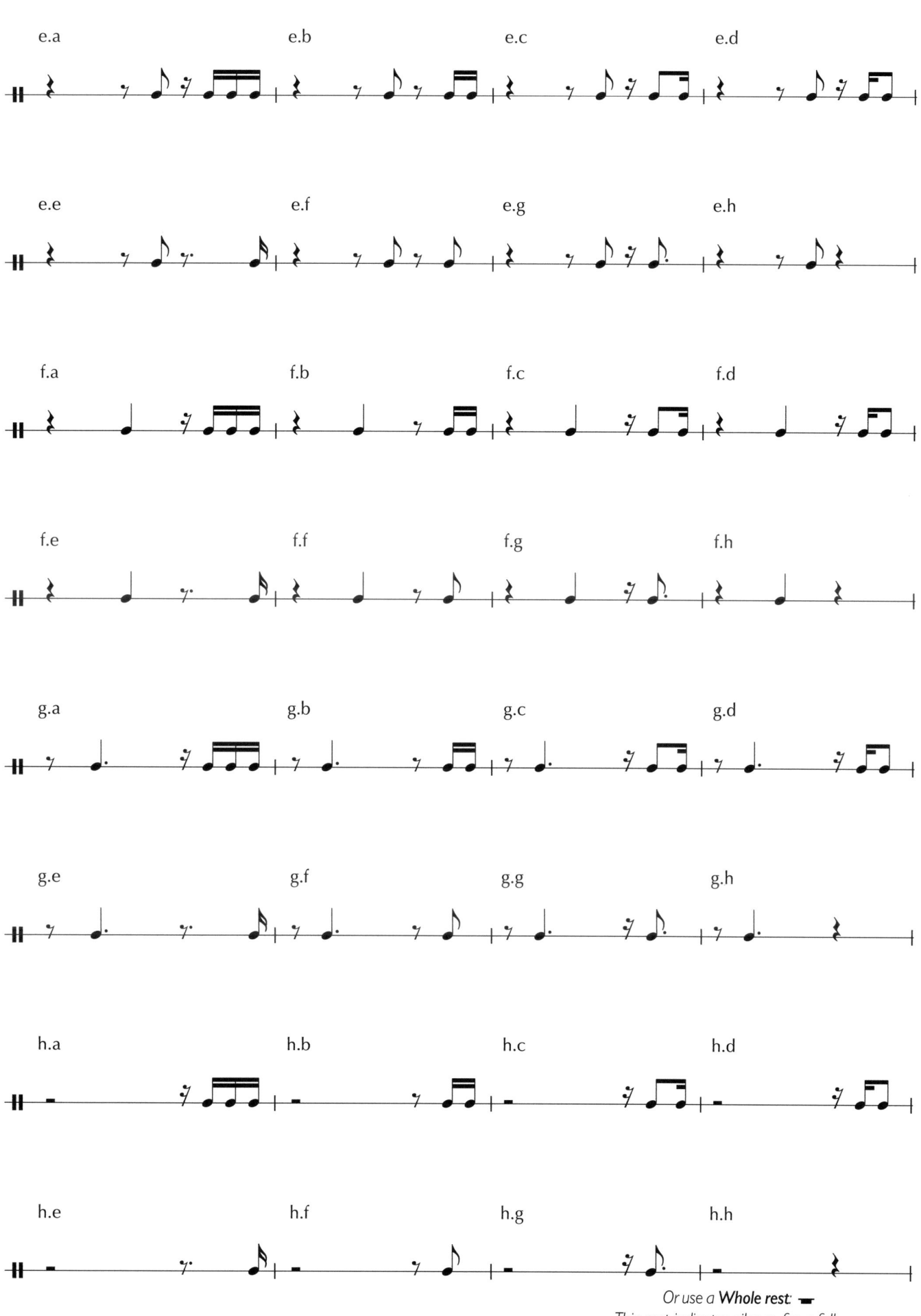

Or use a **Whole rest**: ▬
This rest indicates silence for a full
bar, no matter what time signature it is.

Variation no. 3 (1 + 1 + 1 beats)

Here is a new challenge. We have to see three rhythm-pictures in every bar.

We will use the rhythms from chapter 2. Since they span over one beat only, and we are working with 3/4-time, we will get three rhythm-pictures per bar. One on **each beat** of the bar.

Like this:

By now you probably know that the letters above the bars mainly point to the rhythms in the Basic Exercises and that a **capital letter** points to a Basic Exercise with an A-ending. (1A, 2A etc). And that a small letter points to rhythms with rests or ties.

Since we now have three rhythm-pictures in each bar there are quite many combinations. We won't be able to look at all variations available but hopefully you're getting better and better at recognizing the rhythms in question.

Like before you can get some more exercises by copying the next exercise and put in ties yourself. See next page.

Over to Exercise 3-3(a) on page 86.

Make your own exercises

To save some space in this book I have decided to let you make your own exercises.

Take photo copies of Exercise 3-3(a) on the next page and write **ties** on the copies as follows:

1. Write ties between the rhythm-pictures within the bar. (Var. C):

2. Write ties between the bars. (Var. E)

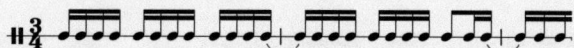

3. Write ties between both the rhythm-pictures within the bar AND between the bars. (Var. G):

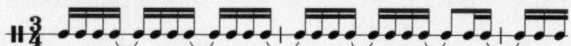

Make a mark on the copy which variation you have choosen: C, E or G.

Note: Exercises 3-2 (B, D and F) don't have ties but rests, so they are still in the book.

Exercise 3-3

A - No TIES (original)

☐ *C - Ties between the rhythm-pictures within the bar*

☐ *E - Ties between the bars*

☐ *G - Ties according to both C and E*

www.khmp.se

Exercise 3-3 cont.

A - No TIES (original)
☐ **C** - Ties between the rhythm-pictures within the bar
☐ **E** - Ties between the bars
☐ **G** - Ties according to both C and E

E.A.A   E.A.B   E.B.C   E.C.D

E.D.E   E.E.F   E.F.G   E.G.H

F.A.A   F.A.B   F.B.C   F.C.D

F.D.E   F.E.F   F.F.G   B.G.H

G.A.A   G.A.B   G.B.C   G.C.D

G.D.E   G.E.F   G.F.G   G.G.H

H.A.A   H.A.B   H.B.C   H.C.D

H.D.E   H.E.F   H.F.G   H.G.H

Exercise 3-3b

Rhythms from Basic Exercise 2a and 2b.

Exercise 3-3b cont.

What you have learned

In chapter 3 you have worked with 3/4-time by combining rhythms from chapter 1 and chapter 2.

You have looked at three ways of viewing the rhythm-pictures:

- as 1 + 2 beats *(with rhythms from chapter 2 and 1).*

- as 2 + 1 beats *(with rhythms from chapter 1 and 2).*

- as 1 +1 +1 beats *(with rhythms from chapter 2).*

Note: In real life you will most likely (between every bar) have to switch between the three ways of viewing that we have covered in this chapter.

CHAPTER

**Combinations from
chapter 1 and chapter 2**
(4/4-time)

Combinations from chapter 1 and chapter 2 (4/4-time)

Let's continue to combine rhythms from chapter 1 and chapter 2 but now in **4/4-time.** *You can read more about time signatures in chapter 11.*

We will start by adding rhythms from chapter 1 in the first part of the bar (two beats) and then two rhythms from chapter 2 on beat three and four.

Like this:

To begin with you might want to see the rhythm-pictures as three parts as depicted above. After some time, you may be able to see them as only two pictures:

As a goal you want to be able to see the two 16th-note rhythms as ONE big picture.

An experienced sight reader can see an entire bar as one single picture or even several bars at once. But that usually takes years of practice. *Just remember to force your eyes to move forward in the music so you don't get stuck in a bar.*

When we combine rhythm-pictures from both chapter 1 and chapter 2 there are a lot of possible combinations of rhythms. We won't be able to go through them all, but hopefully you will be able to recognize these "patterns" when you come across them in the future.

On the next page you can find an instruction on how to expand this chapter by making your own exercises with ties.

Tip: You will soon go to Exercise 4a but before you do that you might want to repeat Basic Exercise 1a (from chapter 1) and Basic Exercise 2a (from chapter 2).

Later on in this chapter you will work with both rests and ties so you may also want to repeat Basic Exercise 1b and Basic Exercise 2b.

As usual the letters A-H (a-h) above a bar point to the rhythm-pictures within that bar.

You can start with a tempo of **70-90 BPM** when doing the exercises in this chapter.

On to Exercise 4a on page 94!

Make your own exercises

To save some space in this book I have decided to let you make your own exercises.

Take photo copies of Exercise 4-1(a) on the next page and write **ties** on the copies as follows:

1. Write ties between the rhythm-pictures within the bar. (Var. C):

2. Write ties between the bars. (Var. E)

3. Write ties between both the rhythm-pictures within the bar AND between the bars. (Var. G):

Make a mark on the copy which variation you have choosen: C, E or G.

Note: Exercises 4-1 (B, D and F) don't have ties but rests, so they are still in the book.

Exercise 4-1

A - No TIES (original)
☐ C - Ties between the rhythm-pictures within the bar
☐ E - Ties between the bars
☐ G - Ties according to both C and E

www.khmp.se

Exercise 4-1 cont.

A - No TIES (original)
☐ C - Ties between the rhythm-pictures within the bar
☐ E - Ties between the bars
☐ G - Ties according to both C and E

MAKE COPIES OF THIS PAGE!
Write TIES according to: C, E or G.

Exercise 4-1b

Rhythms from Basic Exercise 1A and 2B.

Exercise 4-1b cont.

Exercise 4-1d

Rhythms from Basic Exercise 1B and 2A.

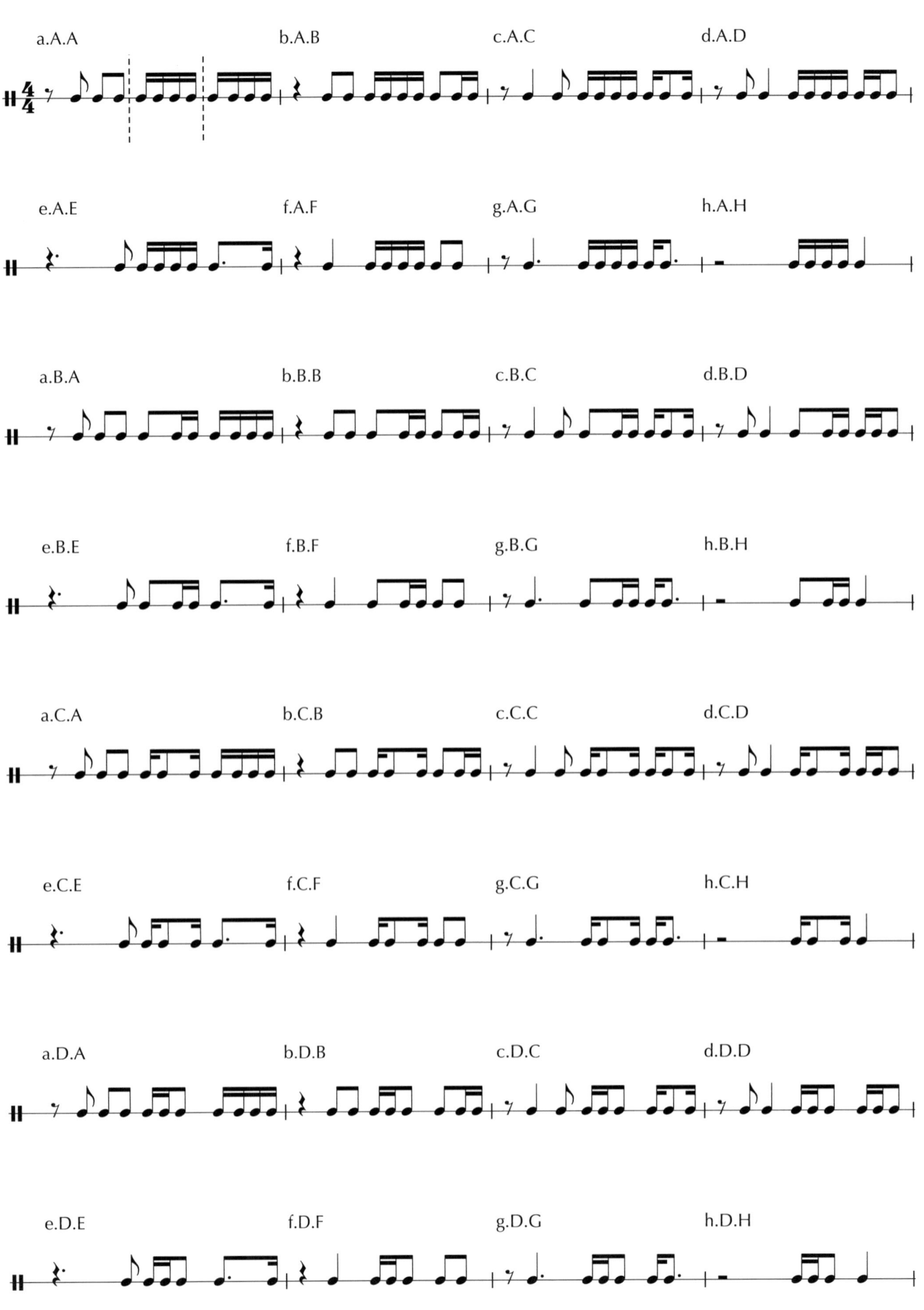

Exercise 4-1d cont.

Exercise 4-1f

Rhythms from Basic Exercise 1B and 2B.

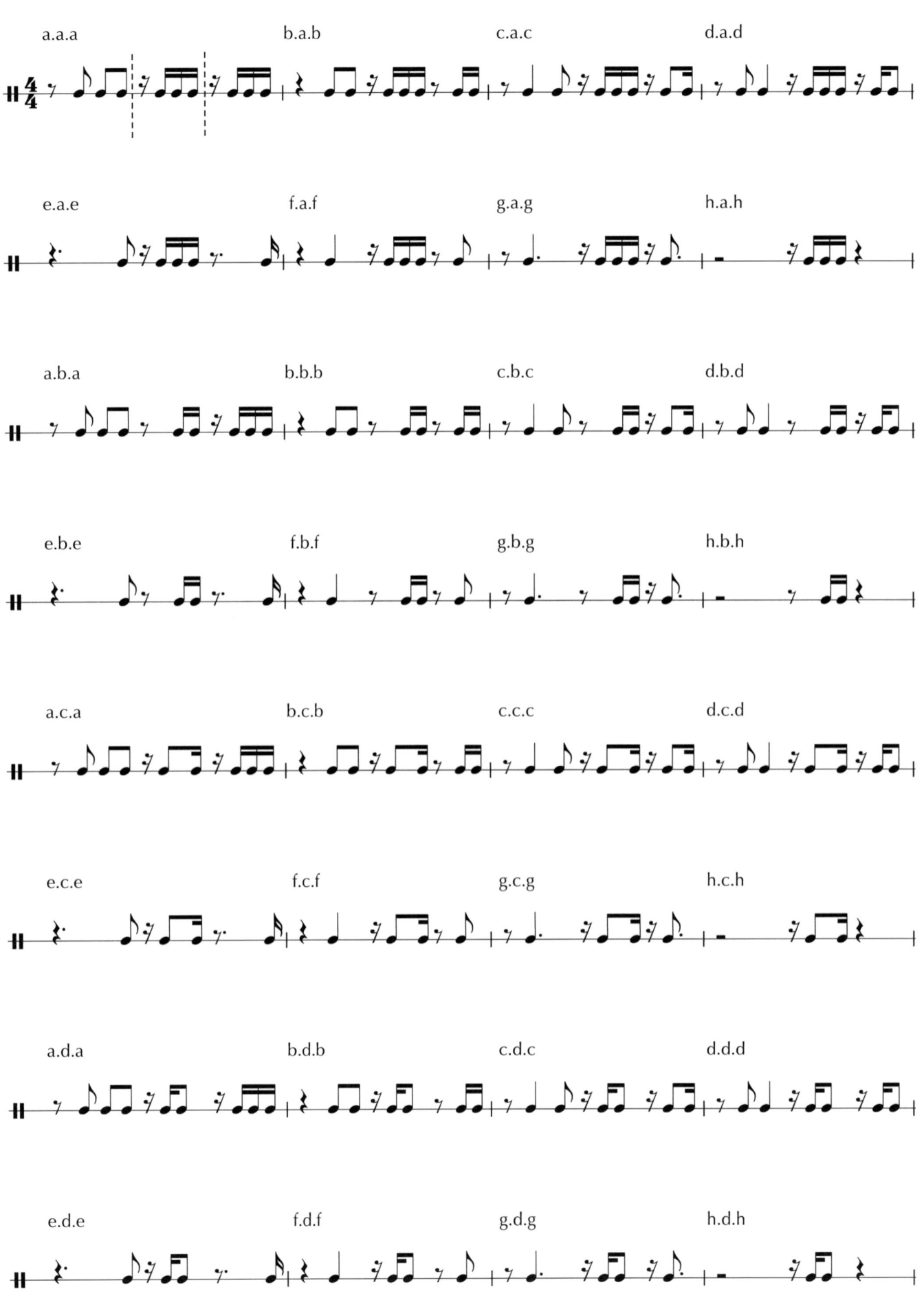

Exercise 4-1f cont.

What you have learned

In chapter 4 you have worked with:

- combinations of rhythms from chapters 1 and 2 in 4/4-time.

Try to follow the study plan at end of the book for a progressive learning curve.

CHAPTER 5

Tuplets – Part 1
Eighth note triplets
Quarter note triplets
Half note triplets

Tuplets – Part 1

In Western music culture it is common with musical elements divisible by two. It is common with 4/4-time, 2/4-time. A verse or chorus is often 8, 16 or 32 bars. We prefer to play note values that can be divided in two, *therefore* our way of writing music is based on halving the note values:

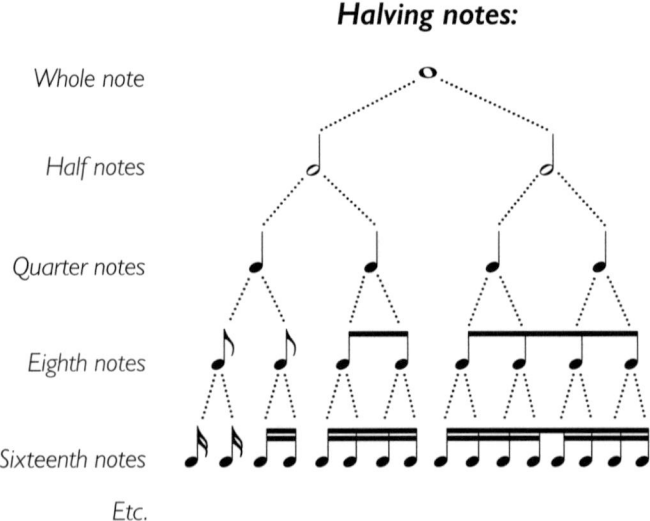

Halving notes:

Whole note

Half notes

Quarter notes

Eighth notes

Sixteenth notes

Etc.

Because of this, we sometimes have trouble with music and note values that don't follow that pattern, for instance **Tuplets** (triplets, quintuplets, septuplets etc). Tuplets are also called **irregular rhythmic groupings**. In this book we will only be looking at **triplets** since that is the most common tuplet.

Triplets

Let's take a closer look at **triplets** in various forms. The word triplet means that instead of two notes over a period of time, there are three. *(Instead of a division of two we have a division of three).*

- A quarter note can be divided into two eighth notes = halving:

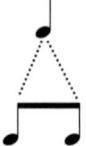

- With a **division of three** on the quarter note you get three **eighth note triplets**:

*Note: Jumping between **halved note values** and **triplets** (or other tuplets) is more difficult.*

Eighth note triplets

We will soon practice rhythms built on three eighth note triplets. They are called that because they look like eighth notes and have the number 3 written above or underneath, and of course because of the division of three instead of two.

We can create four rhythm-pictures from these three eighth note triplets by using ties, just as we did earlier.

Since we only have three notes instead of four, we will only get four rhythms in total. (Instead of eight).

This is how they are created:

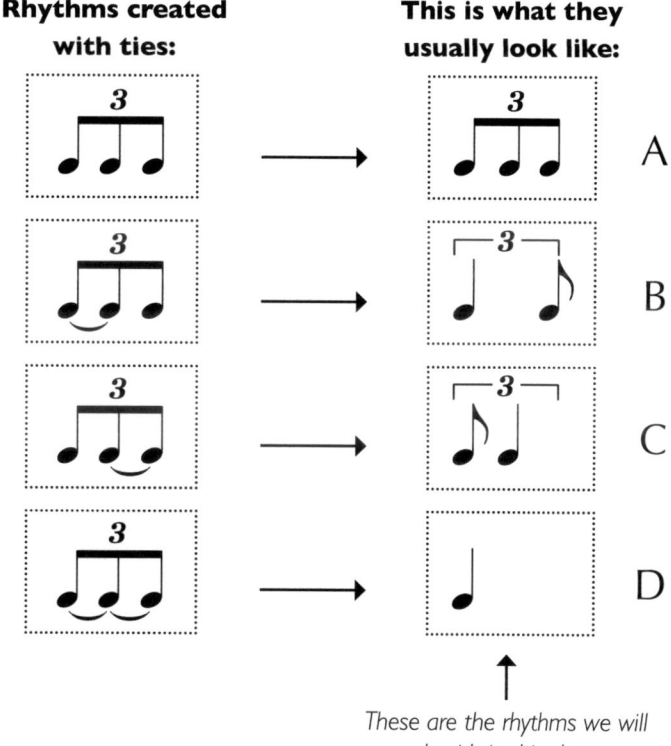

These are the rhythms we will work with in this chapter.

These rhythm-pictures above span over one beat, just as the rhythms in chapter 2. We will be using 2/4-time and place one of the rhythms on the left or the right side in the bars, just as before.

Go to **Basic Exercise 5A** on the next page and learn the rhythm-pictures above in the same manner as in chapter 1 and 2. ⟶

BASIC EXERCISE

5A

IMPORTANT EXERCISE

You can find all Basic Exercises with sound on our website:

www.khmp.se

In this Basic Exercise the bar is divided into two halves by an invisible line, just as in earlier basic Exercises. In the first half you put one of the rhythm-pictures and in the other half is a quarter rest. Like this:

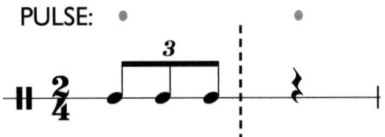

1. Start a metronome or a steady beat at 70-90 BPM (beats per minute).

2. Your teacher sings/plays **rhythm A** below. Student repeats. (While looking at the rhythm). Repeat it until you know it.

3. Go to **rhythm B** and learn it in the same way as rhythm A. Listen and repeat. (While looking at the rhythm).

4. Alternate between rhythm A and B. Don't forget the quarter rest at the end of each bar.

5. Add one rhythm at a time until you have mastered all four rhythms (A-D).

Remember to practice with a steady pulse. (With a metronome or a person playing a steady beat).

Note:
See each rhythm
as a picture!

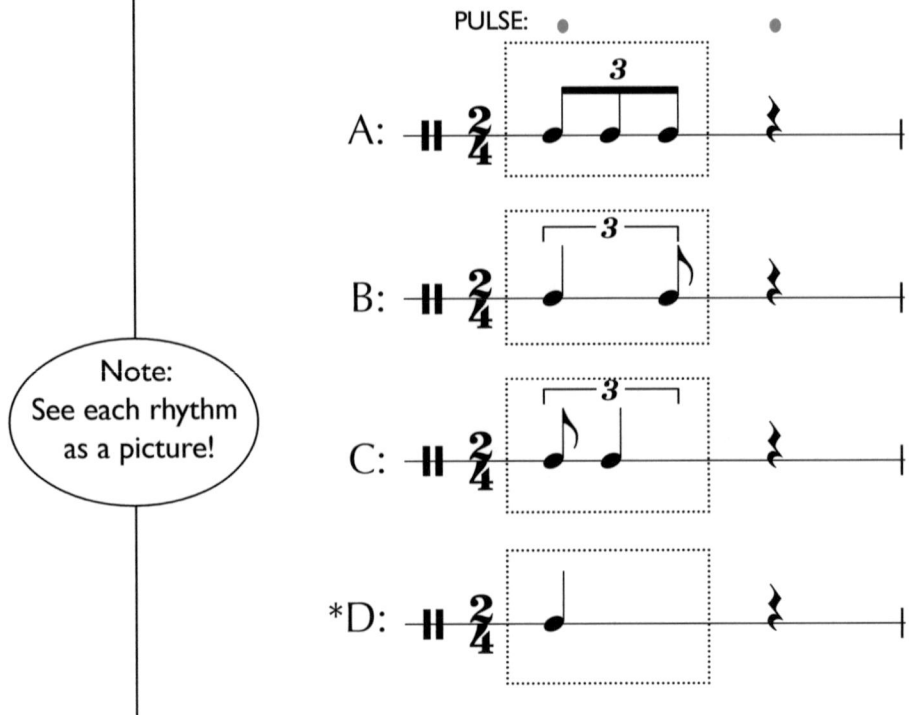

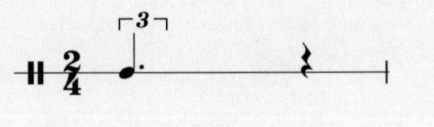

* *In order to be consistent perhaps we should have written rhythm D like this: But in practice this version doesn't exist, hence the quarter note as rhythm D above.*

BEFORE YOU MOVE ON!   When you feel secure playing/singing the rhythms in Basic Exercise 5A you can try Exercise 5a below.

> Remember to divide each bar into two parts and see each rhythm as a picture.

Exercise 5a

Rhythms from Basic Exercise 5A.

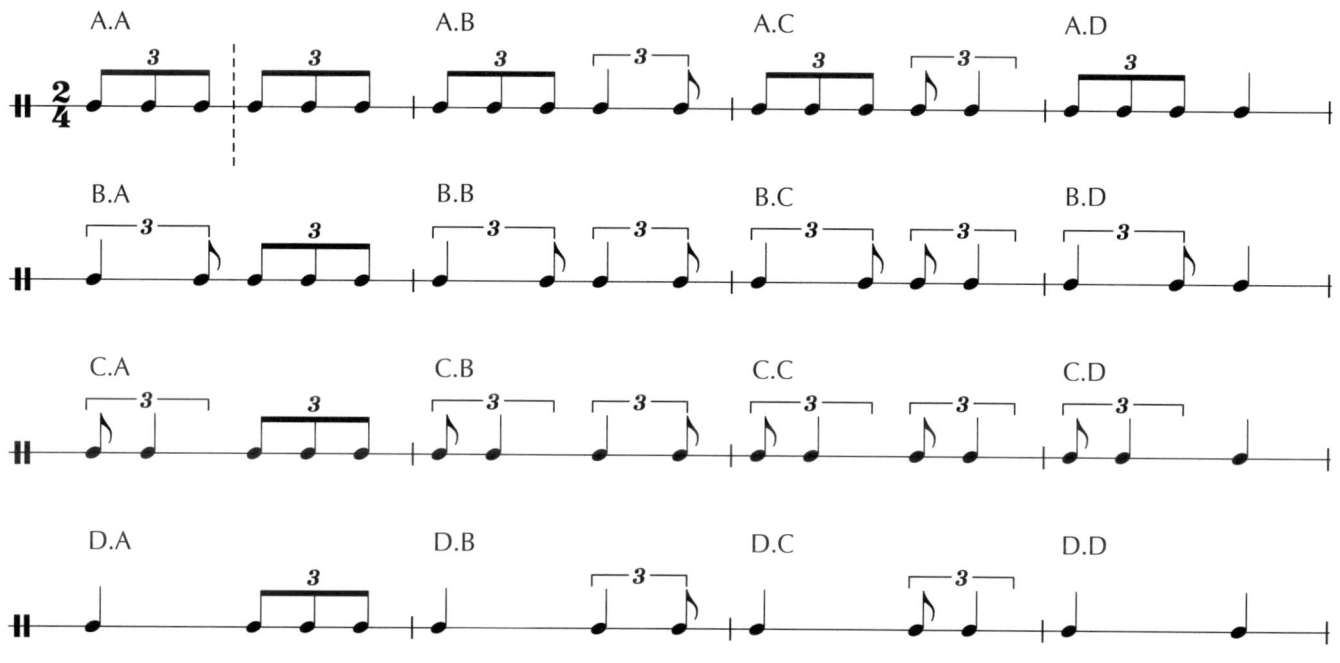

BEFORE YOU MOVE ON!   Before you move on you can jump to chapter 6, page 118.
There you can practise **sixteenth note triplets** in the same way as you just did. *Follow the study plan at the end of the book and you will get a good learning progression.*

Eighth note triplet rests

On the next page you will find Basic Exercise 5B – Rests.
In this exercise you will have the first note in every rhythm-picture replaced by a *rest* of the corresponding value. Learn them in the same way as before.

BASIC EXERCISE
5B
RESTS

IMPORTANT EXERCISE

You can find all Basic Exercises with sound on our website:

www.khmp.se

Note:
See each rhythm
as a picture!

1. Start a metronome or a steady beat at 70-90 BPM (beats per minute).

2. Your teacher sings/plays **rhythm a** below. Student repeats. (While looking at the rhythm). Repeat it until you know it.

3. Go to **rhythm b** and learn it in the same way as rhythm a. Listen and repeat. (While looking at the rhythm).

4. Alternate between rhythm **a** and **b**.
   Don't forget the quarter rest at the end of each bar.

5. Add one rhythm at a time until you have mastered all four rhythms (a-d).

Remember to practice with a steady pulse. (With a metronome or a person playing a steady beat).

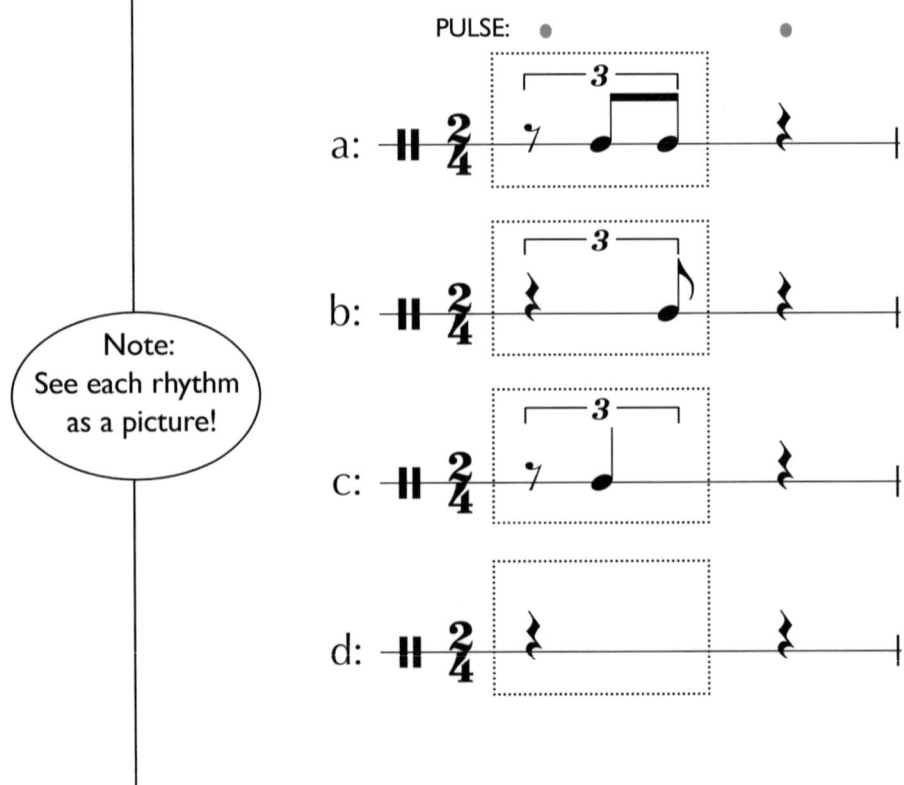

Go to Exercise 5b on the next page. In this Exercise you will learn how to combine rhythms from Basic Exercise 5A and Basic Exercise 5B.

This is followed by Exercise 5c where the rests have been replaced by ties.

On to the Exercises:

> *Remember to divide each bar into two parts and see each rhythm as a picture.*

Exercise 5b

Rhythms from Basic Exercise 5A and 5B.

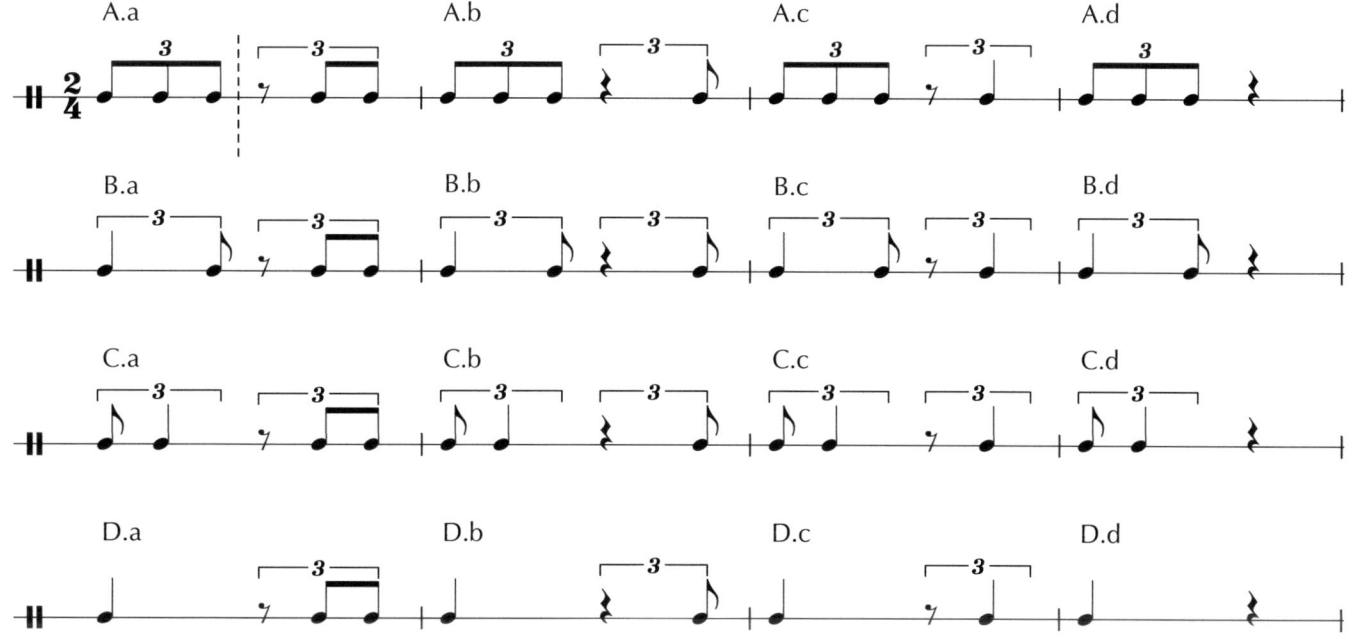

Exercise 5c

Same as Exercise 5b but with ties instead of rests.

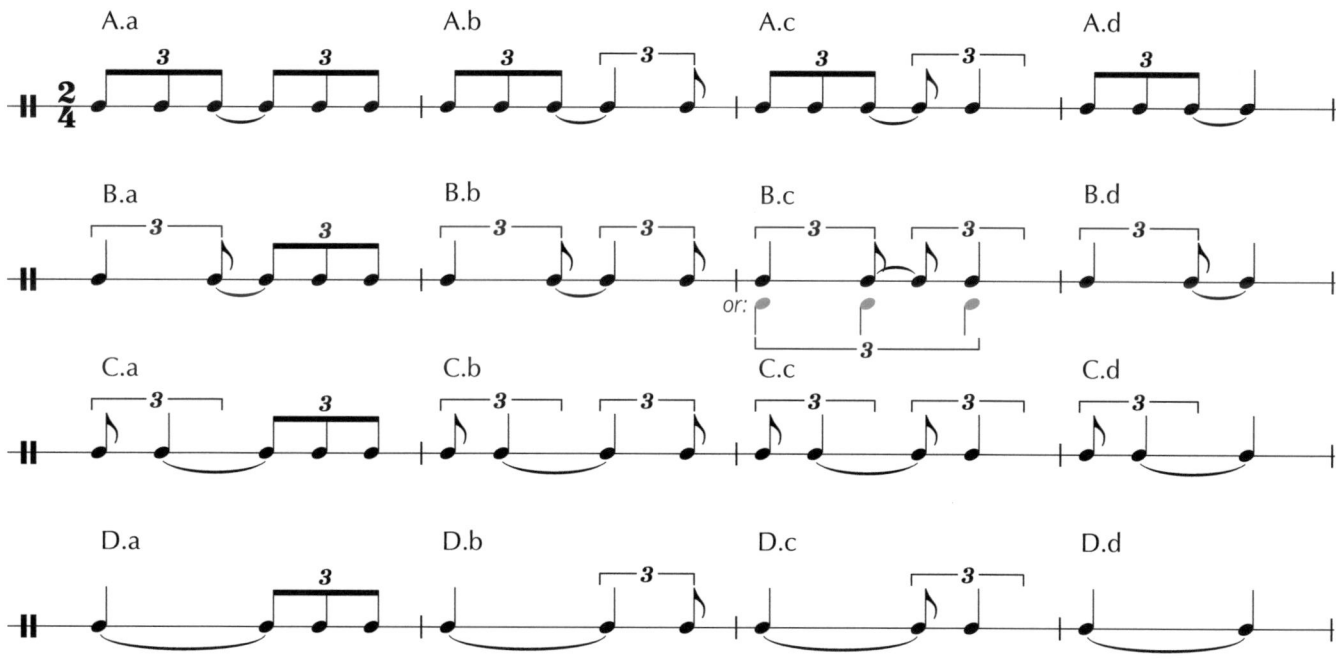

Exercise 5d

Rhythms from Basic Exercise 5B and 5A.

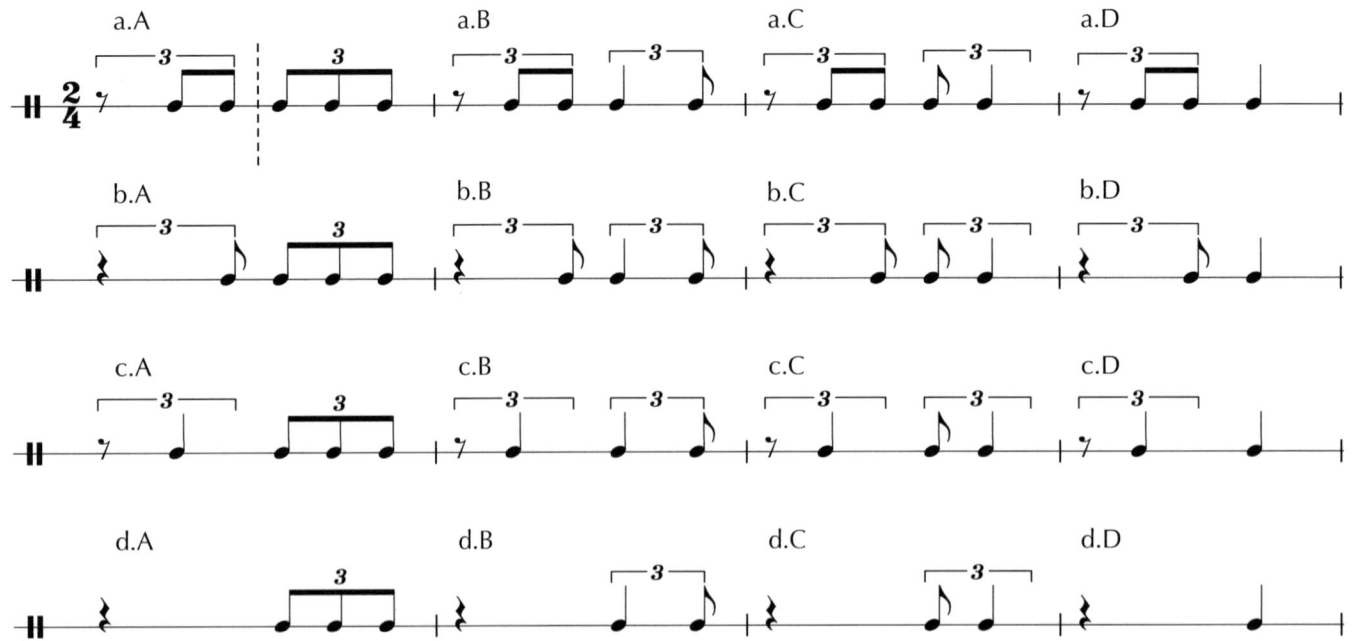

Exercise 5e

Same as Exercise 5d but with ties instead of rests

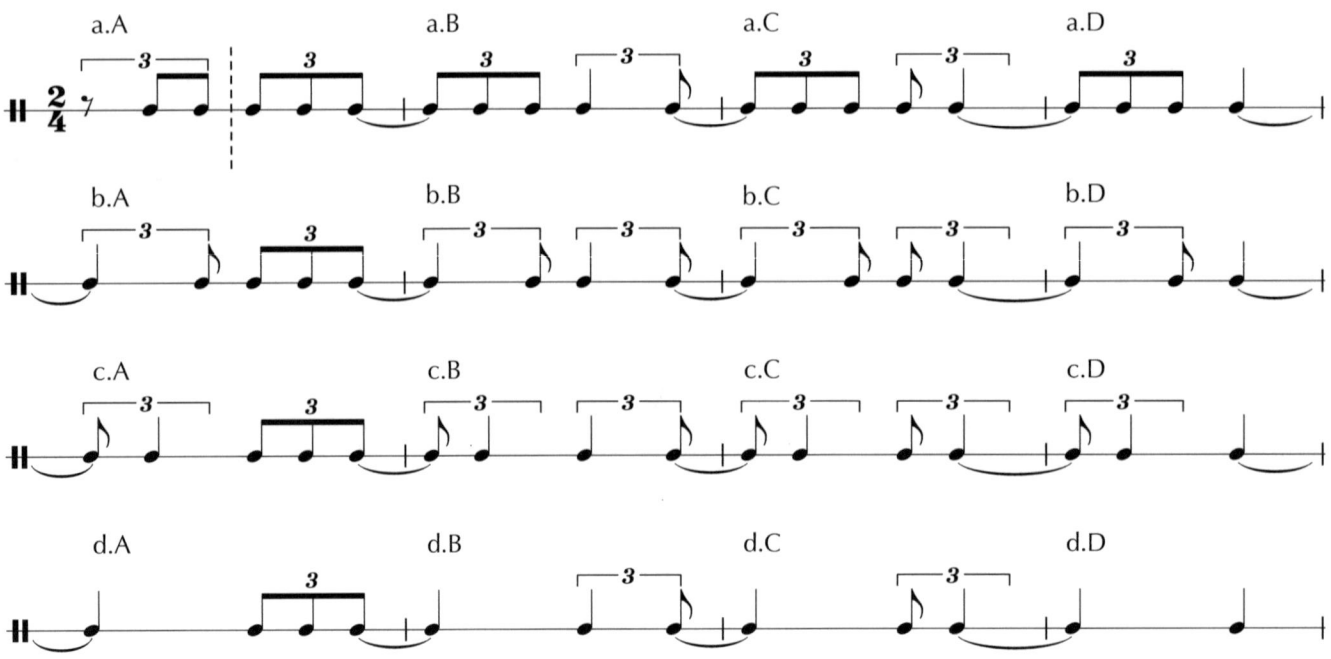

Exercise 5f

Rhythms from Basic Exercise 5B.

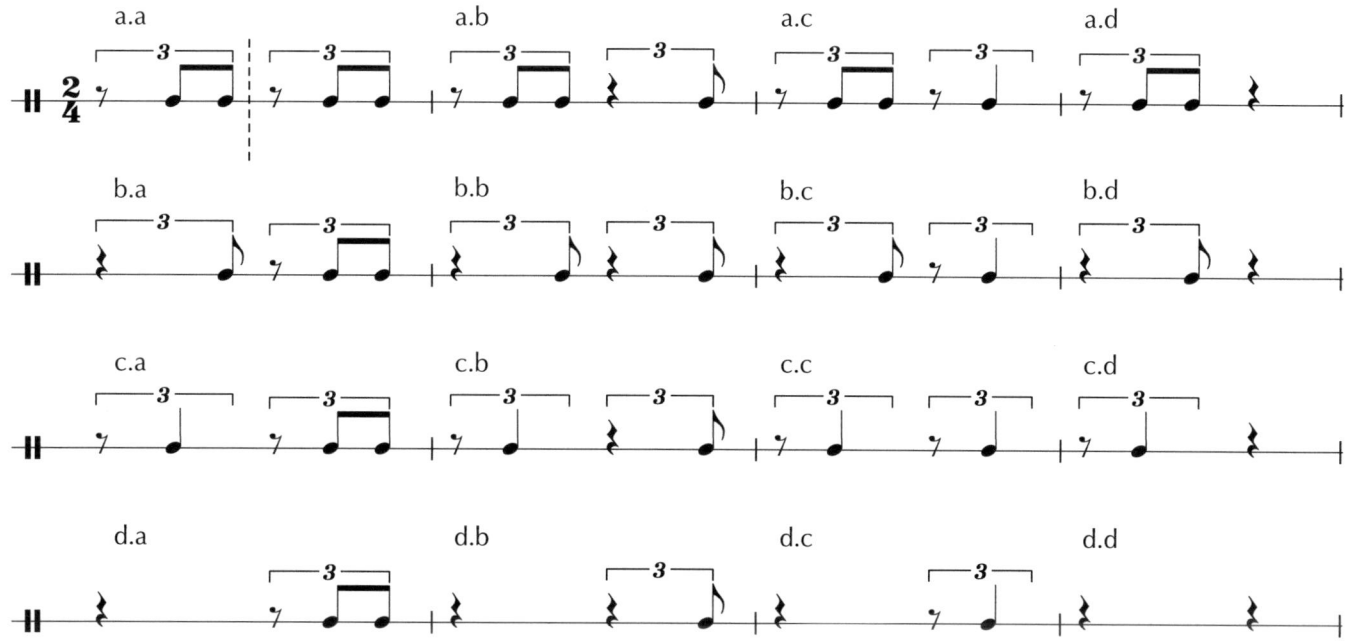

Exercise 5g

Same as Exercise 5f but with ties instead of rests

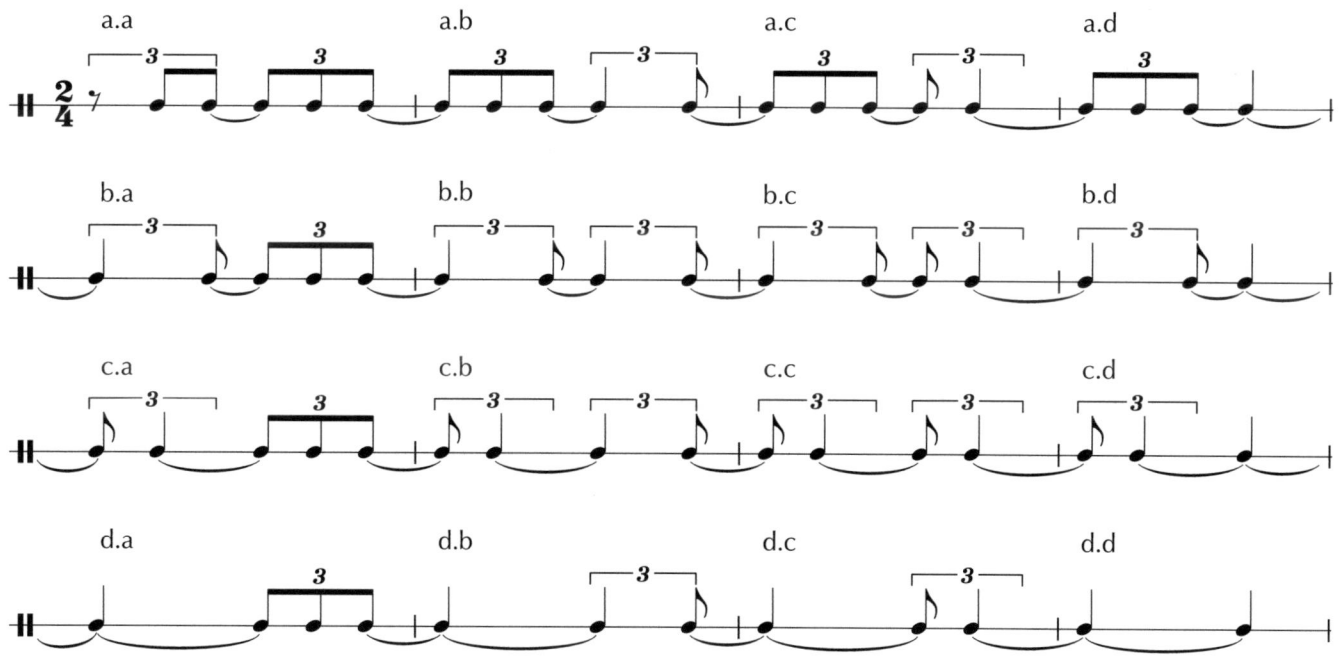

Quarter note triplets

Quarter note triplets come from dividing a half note in three, instead of two. (Look at the beginning of this chapter).

It is tempting to do as we did with the eighth note triplets; to make four rhythm-pictures, call them A-D, and learn them by ear. (Just as earlier). I am sure that would have worked fine too, but instead we are going to use another approach that will make these quarter note triplets easier and more comfortable to perform.

In bar 7 in Exercise 5c on page 109, you can see three quarter note triplets as an alternative. They are exactly that; *an alternative to eighth note triplets with ties!*

It's often better to use larger note values instead of smaller ones with ties. That is also true when it comes to quarter note triplets. Still, it is good to subdivide the quarter note triplets into eigth note triplets to make them easier to perform.

TRIPLET STUDY #1

IMPORTANT EXERCISE

Here is a triplet study in five steps. The goal is to play the quarter note triplets correctly in step 5. There you can see the most common way to write three quarter note triplets. Begin with step 1 and continue to step 5. *Note that step 4 and 5 sound identical.*

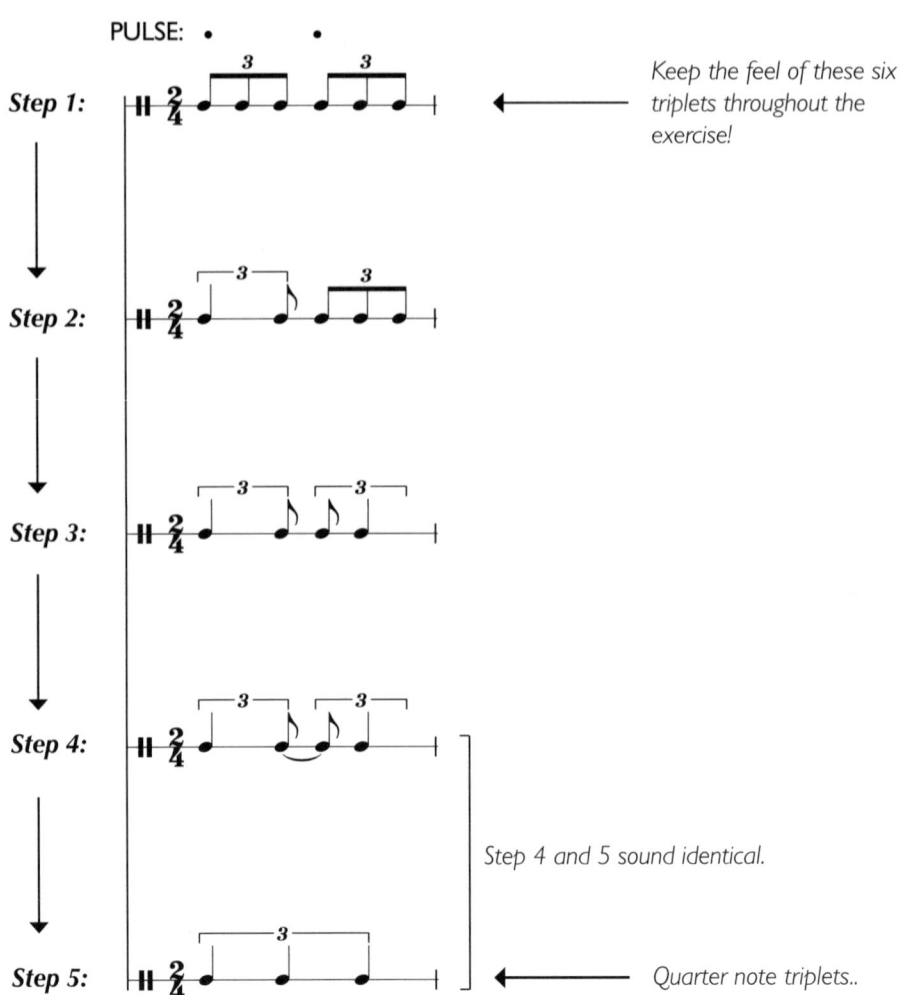

PULSE:

Step 1:

Keep the feel of these six triplets throughout the exercise!

Step 2:

Step 3:

Step 4:

Step 4 and 5 sound identical.

Step 5:

Quarter note triplets..

Here are some common quarter note triplet (based) rhythms:

You can also find rhythms that are a mixture of quarter note triplets and eighth note triplets:

These rhythm-pictures can be a bit confusing, but by having the eighth note triplet as a foundation you will be able to sort them out. It is important that you know your eighth note triplets before you go to triplet study #2 where we will study rhythms where some are a mixture of quarter note triplets and eighth note triplets.

TRIPLET STUDY #2

IMPORTANT EXERCISE

In the left column below, you see eighth note triplet rhythms from Basic Exercise 5A that have been tied together. And to the right you see how these rhythms can be written as a mixture of eighth note triplets and quarter note based triplets.

Play each row in the exercise until you are comfortable with both versions. Then you can jump to Exercise 5c alt.2 on the next page, which is identical to Exercise 5c on page 109, but now written using the rhythms to the right below when possible.

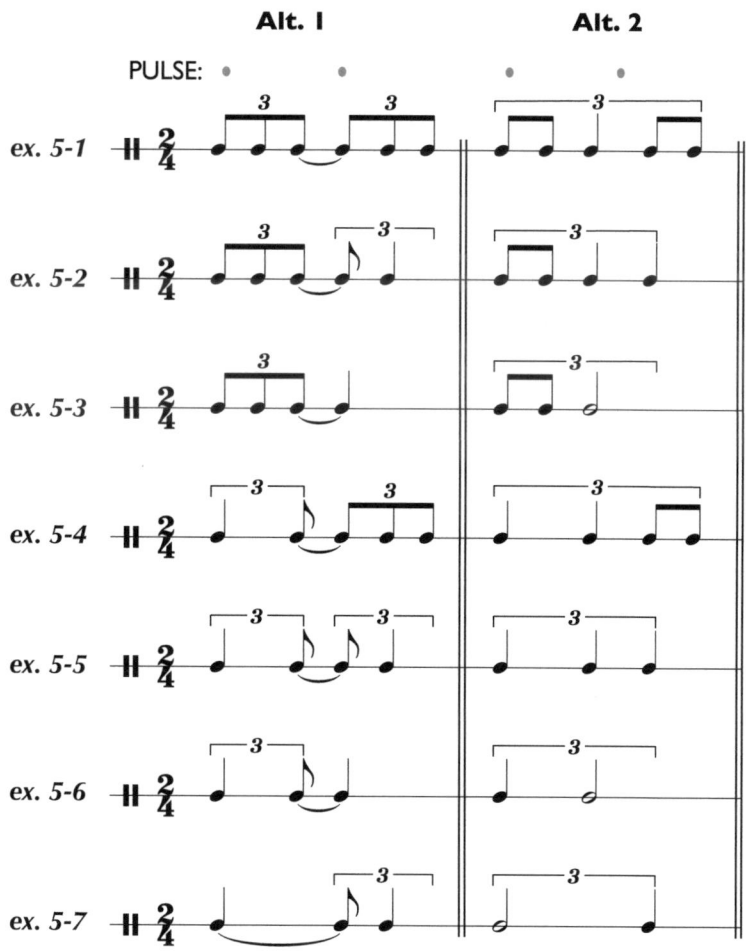

Exercise 5c alt.2

Same as Exercise 5c but with rhythm-pictures based on quarter note triplets when possible.

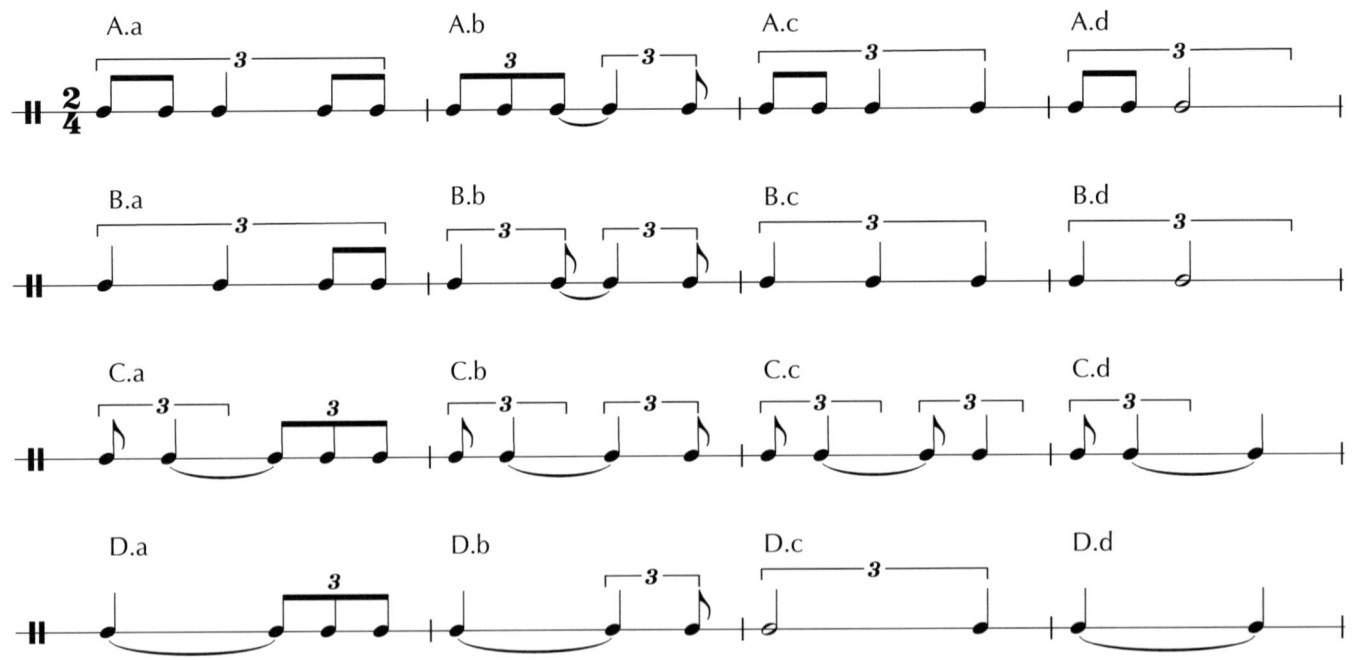

Exercise 5g alt.2

Same as Exercise 5g but with rhythm-pictures based on quarter note triplets when possible.

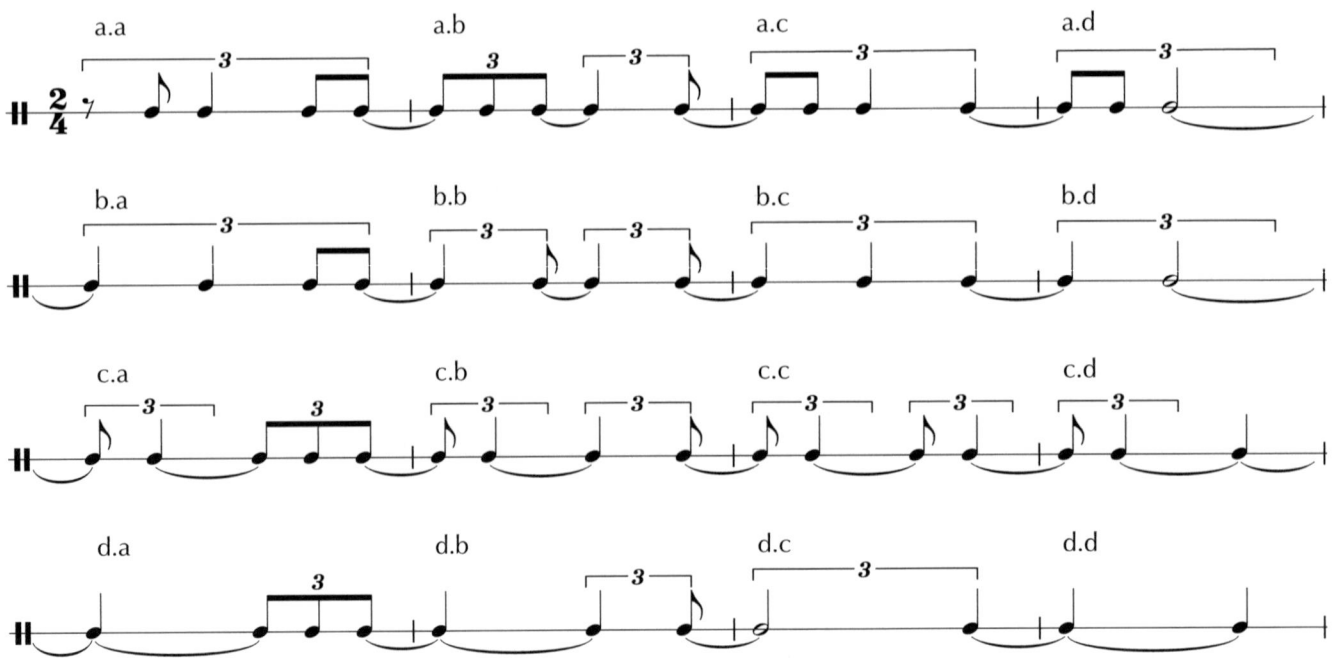

Half note triplets

If you take a whole note and divide it in three you get half note triplets. This means you must play three evenly spaced notes over four beats. This can be very hard to do but I'll show you a trick on how to manage them.

All triplet notes can be divided in two. If you do that with a half note triplet note you get quarter note triplets. And if you divide quarter note triplets you get eight note triplets etc. Subdividing to a smaller triplet underneath a larger one can usually help you play them correctly.

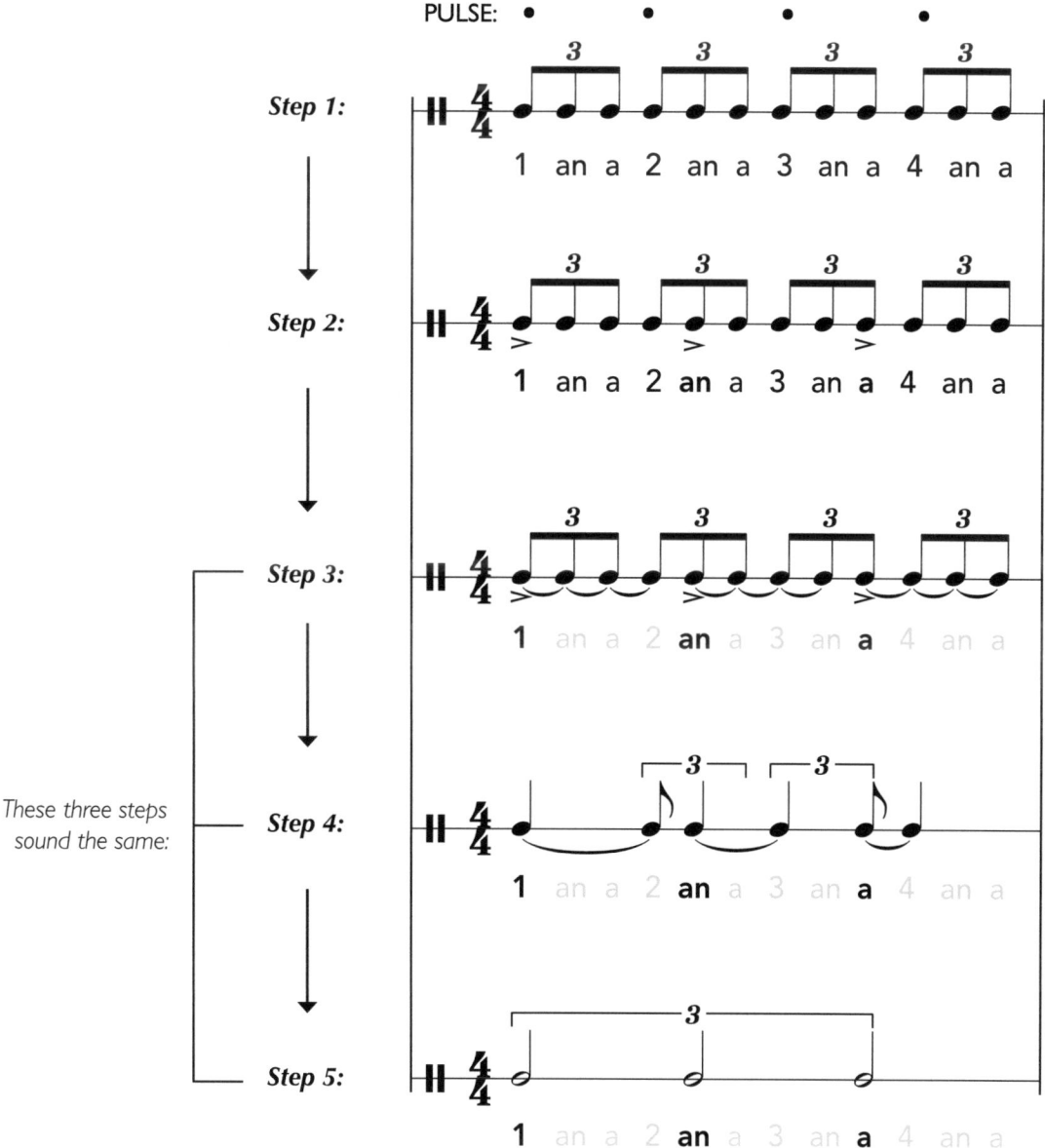

TRIPLET STUDY #3
HALF NOTE TRIPLETS

IMPORTANT EXERCISE

Let's do triplet study #3 so that you can perform half note triplets correctly. This exercise is in 5 steps. Step 1 starts with a whole bar of eighth note triplets. In step 2 you will add an **accent** on every fourth note: 1 an a 2 **an** a 3 an **a** 4 an a

In step 3 we have tied together groups of four notes, as marked with accent in step 2. Step 4 will show you another familiar way of seeing them. And finally in step 5 you see the half note triplets – our goal. Note that step 3, 4 and 5 sound identical.

What you have learned

In chapter 5 you have worked with:

- irregular rhythmic groupings called tuplets *(in this case TRIPLETS)*.

- looked at the difference between halving notes and dividing them in three.

- Basic Exercises 5A and 5B, based on eighth note triplets.

- how to create quarter note triplets from eighth note triplets

- worked with embedded eighth note triplets in quarter note based triplets

- created half note triplets from eighth note triplets.

CHAPTER 6

Tuplets – Part 2
Sixteenth note triplets

Sixteenth note triplets

We will now look at rhythms based on three sixteenth note triplets.

The number three above the notes indicates that you now can fit three notes in the same space as two. Since we only have three notes as a starting point, we only get four different rhythms to memorize:

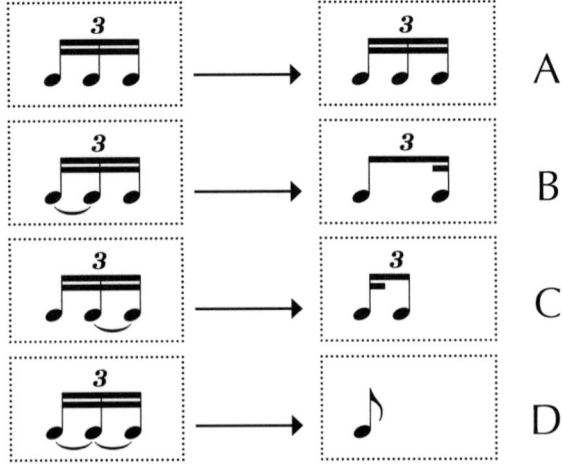

A

B

C

D

Note that the pulse now is eighth notes, and the time signature is 2/8-time.

Split the bar in two and put one rhythm-picture on the first beat (first half) and an eighth note rest on the second beat (second half).

1. Start a metronome or a steady beat at 80-90 BPM (beats per minute).

2. Your teacher sings/plays rhythm A below. Student repeats. (While looking at the rhythm). Repeat it until you know it.

3. Add one rhythm at a time until you have mastered all four rhythms (A-D).

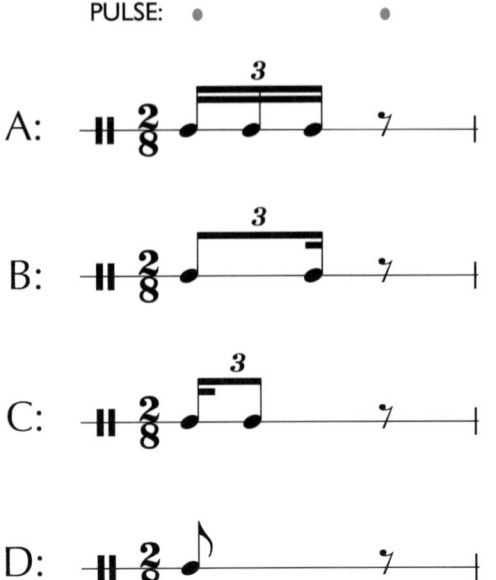

Exercise 6

A - No TIES (original)

❑ C - *Ties between the rhythm-pictures within the bar*

❑ E - *Ties between the bars*

❑ G - *Ties according to both C and E*

MAKE COPIES OF THIS PAGE!
Write TIES according to: C, E or G.

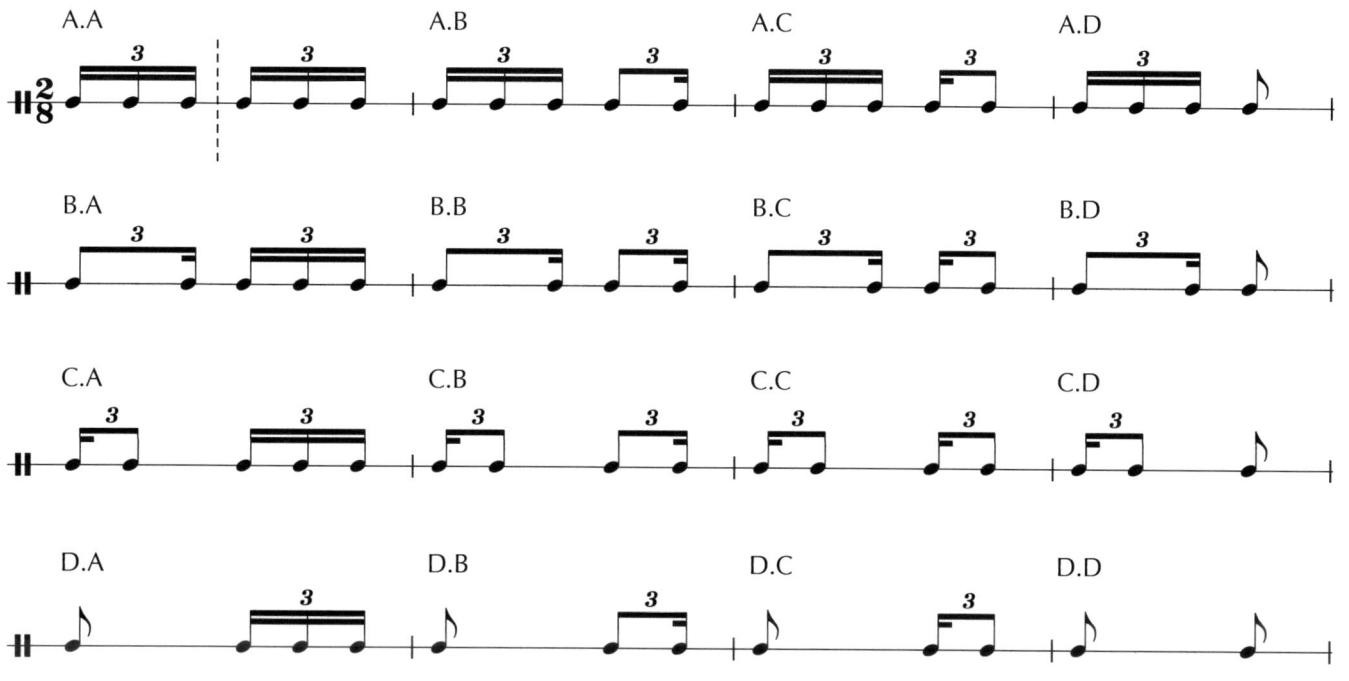

Make your own exercises

To save some space in this book I have decided to let you make your own exercises.

Take photo copies of Exercise 6 above and write **ties** on the copies as follows:

1. Write ties between the rhythm-pictures within the bar. (Var. C):

2. Write ties between the bars. (Var. E)

3. Write ties between both the rhythm-pictures within the bar AND between the bars. (Var. G):

Make a mark on the copy which variation you have choosen: C, E or G.

BASIC EXERCISE
6B
RESTS

IMPORTANT EXERCISE

You can find all Basic Exercises with sound on our website:

www.khmp.se

In Basic Exercise 6B we will replace the first note in each rhythm with a **rest** of the corresponding value. We still have 2/8-time, so the pulse is eighth notes.

1. Start a metronome or a steady beat at 80-90 BPM (beats per minute).

2. Your teacher sings/plays **rhythm A** below. Student repeats. (While looking at the rhythm). Repeat it until you know it.

3. Add one rhythm at a time until you have mastered all four rhythms (A-D).

Remember to see each rhythm as a picture!

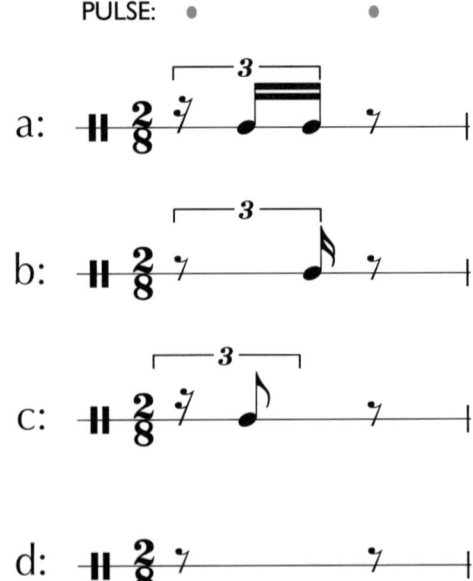

Exercise 6b

Rhythms from Basic Exercises 6a and 6b.

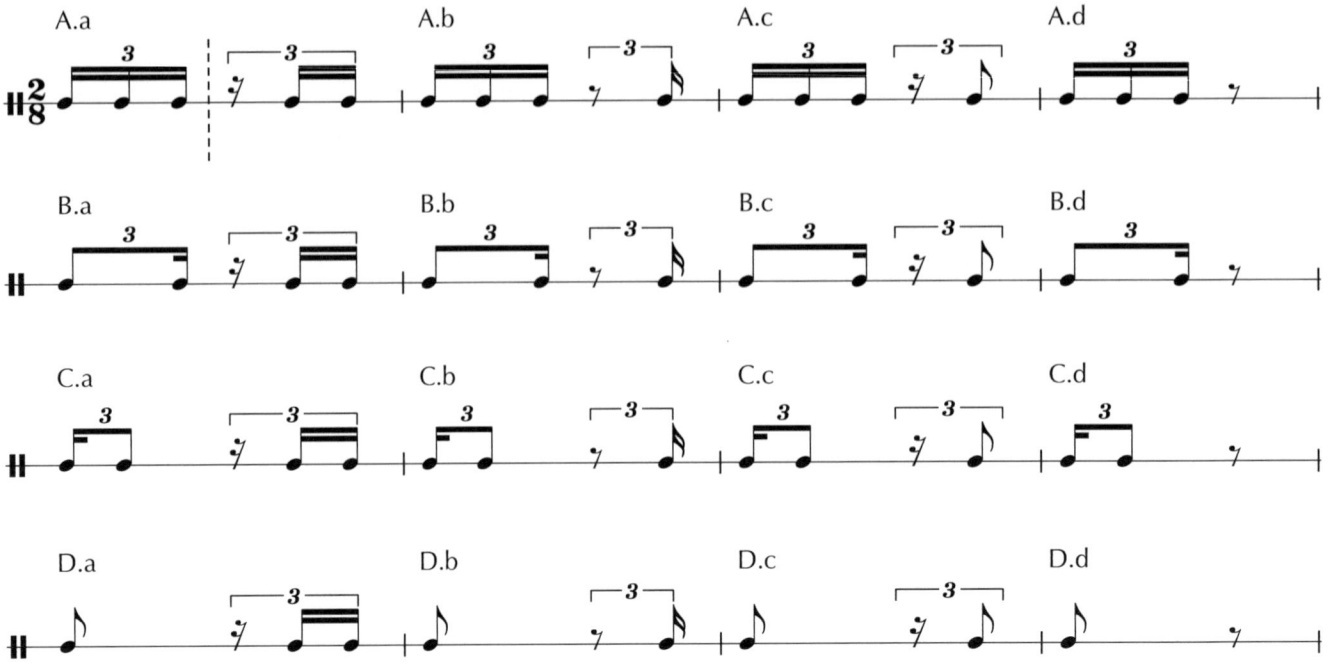

Exercise 6d

Rhythms from Basic Exercises 6b and 6a.

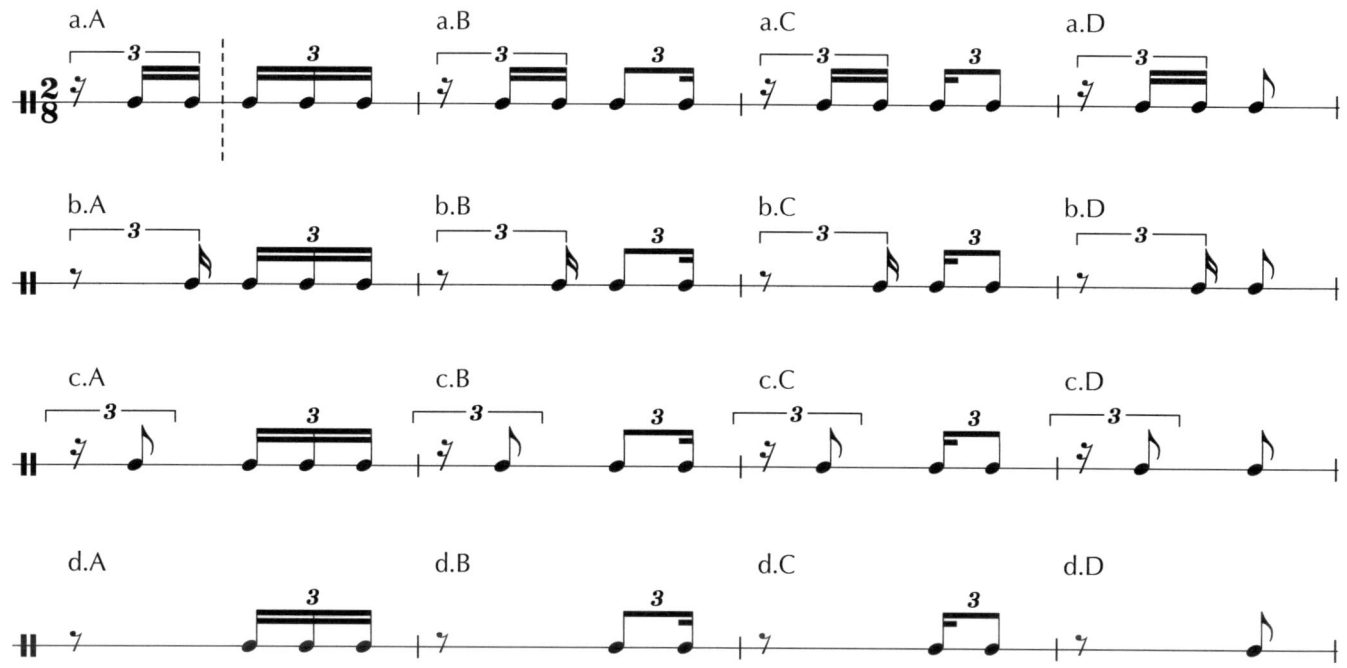

Exercise 6f

Rhythms from Basic Exercise 6b.

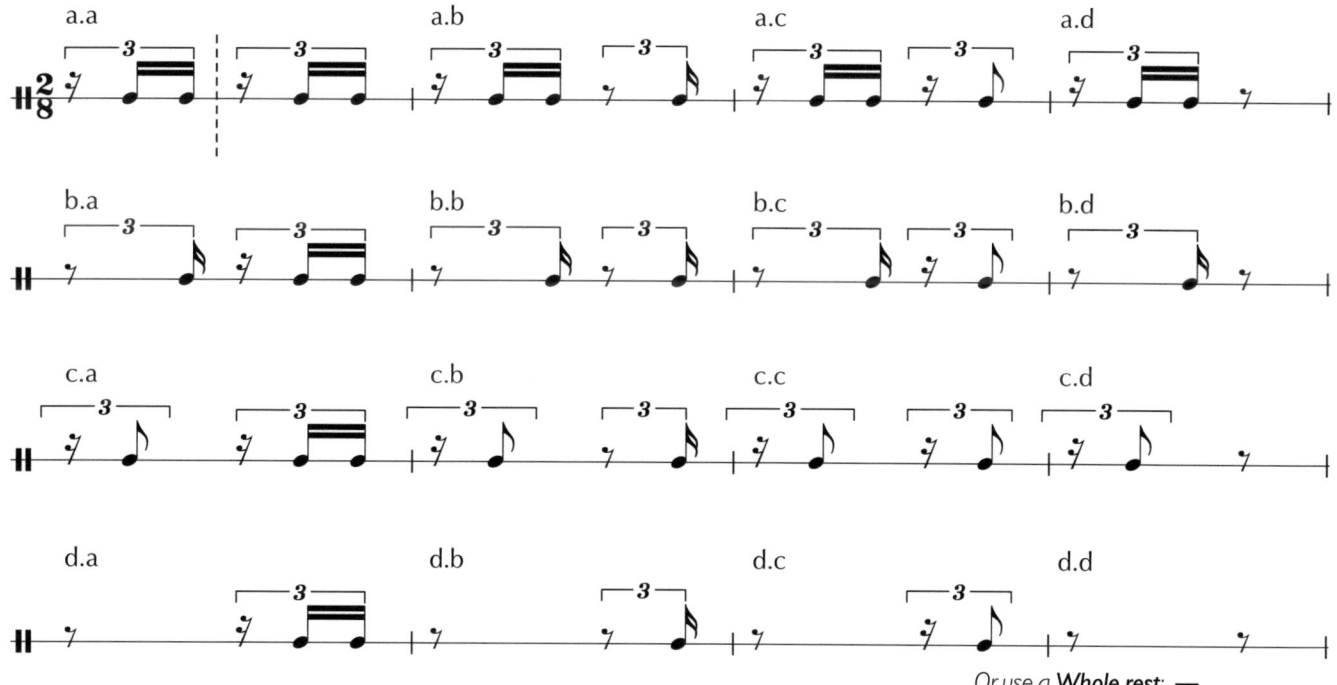

*Or use a **Whole rest**:* ▬
This rest indicates silence for a full bar,
no matter what time signature it is.

Sixteenth note triplets mixed with eighth note triplets

At page 113 in chapter 5, you could see rhythms with both quarter note triplets *and* eighth note triplets together. Like this:

Now we'll explore rhythm pictures with **sixteenth note triplets** mixed together with **eighth note triplets**.

TRIPLET STUDY #4

IMPORTANT EXERCISE

In this triplet study you will see some common ways of writing tied sixteenth and eighth note triplets.

In the left column (bar) below you will find two rhythm pictures from Basic Exercise 6A, tied together. And in the right column (bar) you will find the same rhythms rewritten with sixteenth note triplets and eighth note triplets. This will remove the ties which sometimes makes it easier to read. On the other hand, ties can make you *understand* the rhythms better.

Practice each row (exercise) below until you have mastered both ways of reading the rhythms. Then you can move on to the exercises on the next page that uses the rhythms in the right column below.

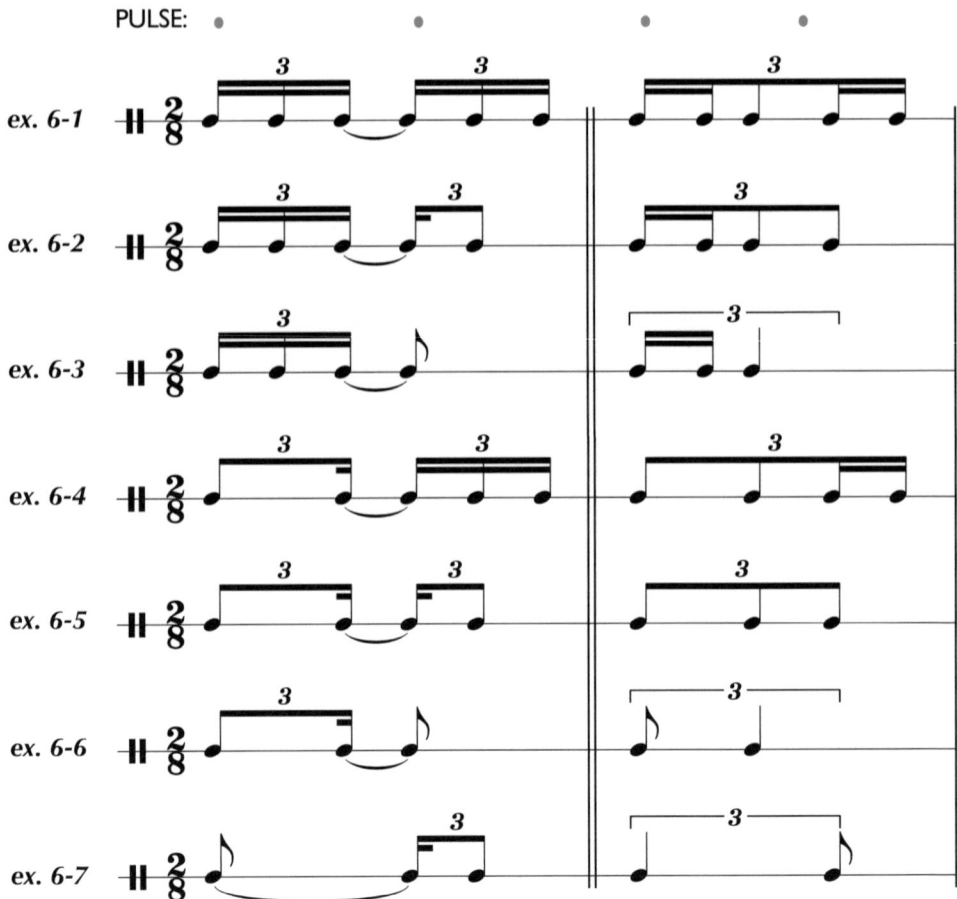

Exercise 6c alt.2

Same as Exercise 6c but with eighth note triplets when possible.

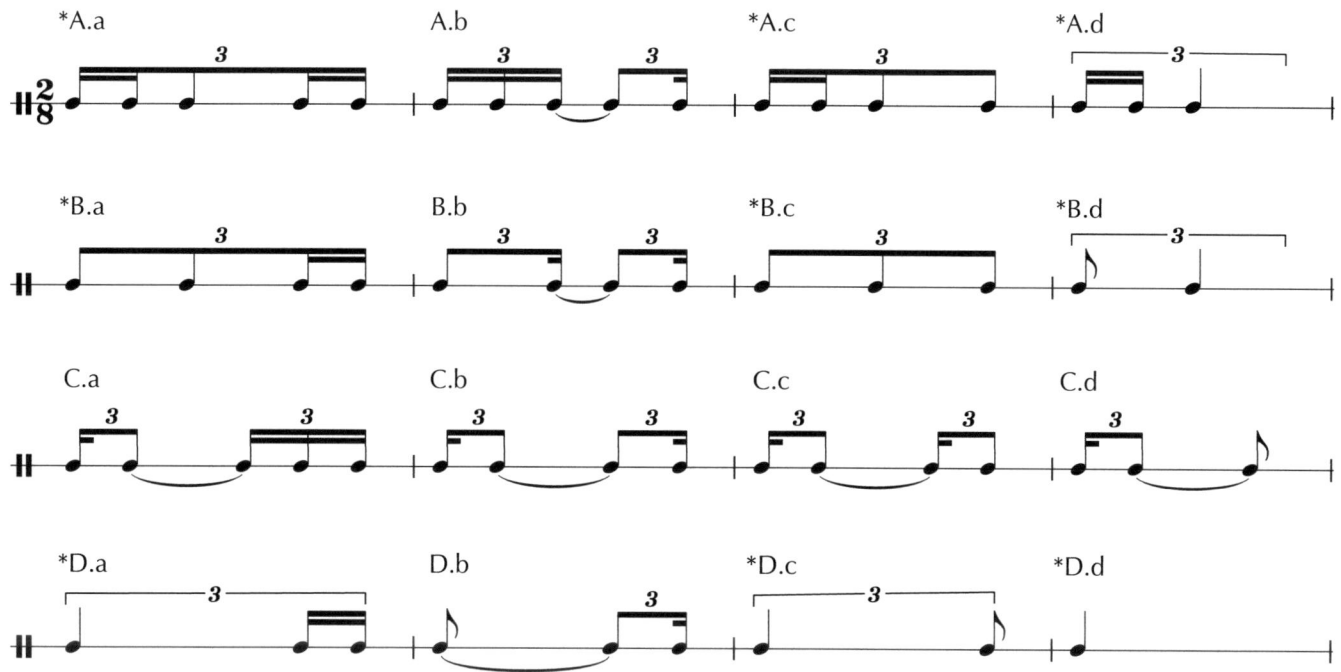

Note: *You create Exercise 6c yourself! See p. 119.*

Exercise 6g alt.2

Same as Exercise 6g but with eigth note triplets when possible.

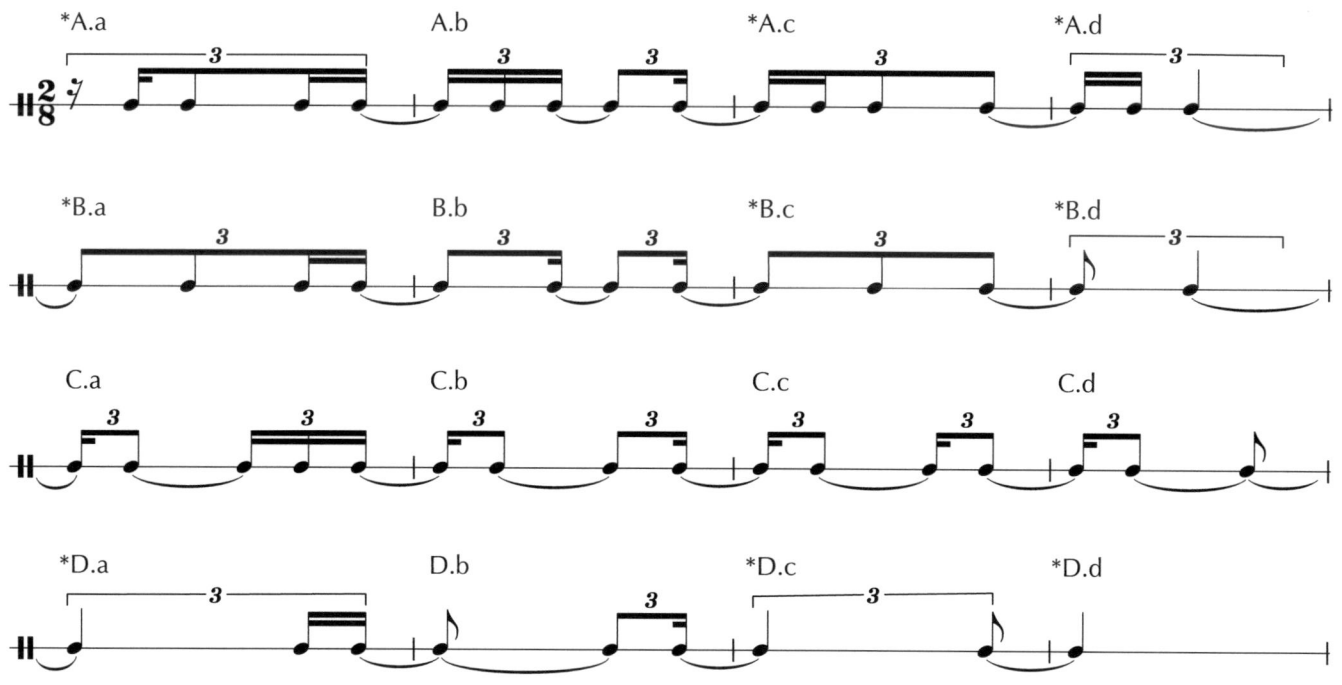

* *These rhythm-pictures are rewritten according to the principle on page 122. Not applicable to D.d which is rewritten in another way).*

Note: *You create Exercise 6g yourself! See p. 119.*

What you have learned

In chapter **6** you have:

- worked with triplets in Basic Exercise **6A**.

- worked with triplets and rests in Basic Exercise **6B**.

- looked at how eighth note triplets appear when they are mixed with sixteenth note triplets.

CHAPTER 7

**Combinations of triplets
and other note values**

Combinations of triplets and other note values

In this chapter we will combine triplets with note values from earlier chapters. One of the hardest things for most of us is the transition from even note values to triplets (or other tuplets).

We will start off by using rhythms from Basic Exercise 1A in the first half of the bars and triplet rhythms from Basic Exercise 5A in the second half. Like this:

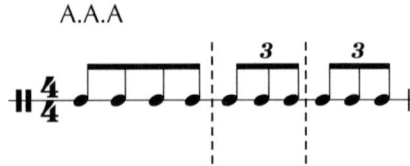

To begin with you can try to see three rhythms per bar but later you may be able to see both triplet rhythms as one whole.

Have a metronome going at 70-85 BPM during the following exercises.

PRE-EXERCISE 1

To familiarize yourself with the transitions mentioned above you can repeat bar one in the exercise below (same as above) for a while before you move on.

Exercise 7-1a

Rhythms from Basic Exercises 1a and 5a.

Exercise 7-1b

Rhythms from Basic Exercises 1a and 5b.

Exercise 7-1c

Same as Exercise 7b but with ties instead of rests.

* *Rewritten to other note values, instead of using ties.*

Sixteenth notes in combination with eighth note triplets

Let's look at combinations of rhythms derived from chapter 2 (sixteenth notes) and triplets from chapter 5. Make sure you know the rhythms from these chapters before you move on.

PRE-EXERCISE 2

Here is a warm up exercise where you familiarize yourself with the transition between sixteenth notes and eighth note triplets.

Tempo: 60-90 BPM

Make your own exercises

To save some space in this book I have decided to let you make your own exercises.

Take photo copies of Exercise 7-2 on the next page and write **ties** on the copies as follows:

1. Write ties between the rhythm-pictures within the bar. (Var. C):

2. Write ties between the bars. (Var. E)

3. Write ties between both the rhythm-pictures within the bar AND between the bars. (Var. G):

Make a mark on the copy which variation you have choosen: C, E or G.

- Play the following exercises at different tempi, like:
  56 BPM, 70 BPM and 90 BPM.

- You can also try to use an eighth note pulse = 4/8-time.

Exercise 7-2

A - No TIES (original)

☐ *C - Ties between the rhythm-pictures within the bar*

☐ *E - Ties between the bars*

☐ *G - Ties according to both C and E*

Exercise 7-2b

Rhythms from Basic Exercises 5a and 2b.

Exercise 7-2d

Rhythms from Basic Exercises 5b and 2a.

Exercise 7-2f

Rhythms from Basic Exercises 5b and 2b.

Sixteenth notes and sixteenth note triplets

On the next page you will find an exercise with rhythms from Basic Exercise 2a and Basic Exercise 6a. The exercise is in 3/8-time so start with an eighth note pulse at 110 BPM. You can later try with one beat per bar = more difficult. You will practice more of dotted quarter note pulse in chapters 9 and 10.

Note how the rhythms are beamed together. This is common in 3/8, 6/8 and 9/8-time etc. (See chapter 10).

Exercise 7-3a

Rhythms from Basic Exercises 2a and 6a.

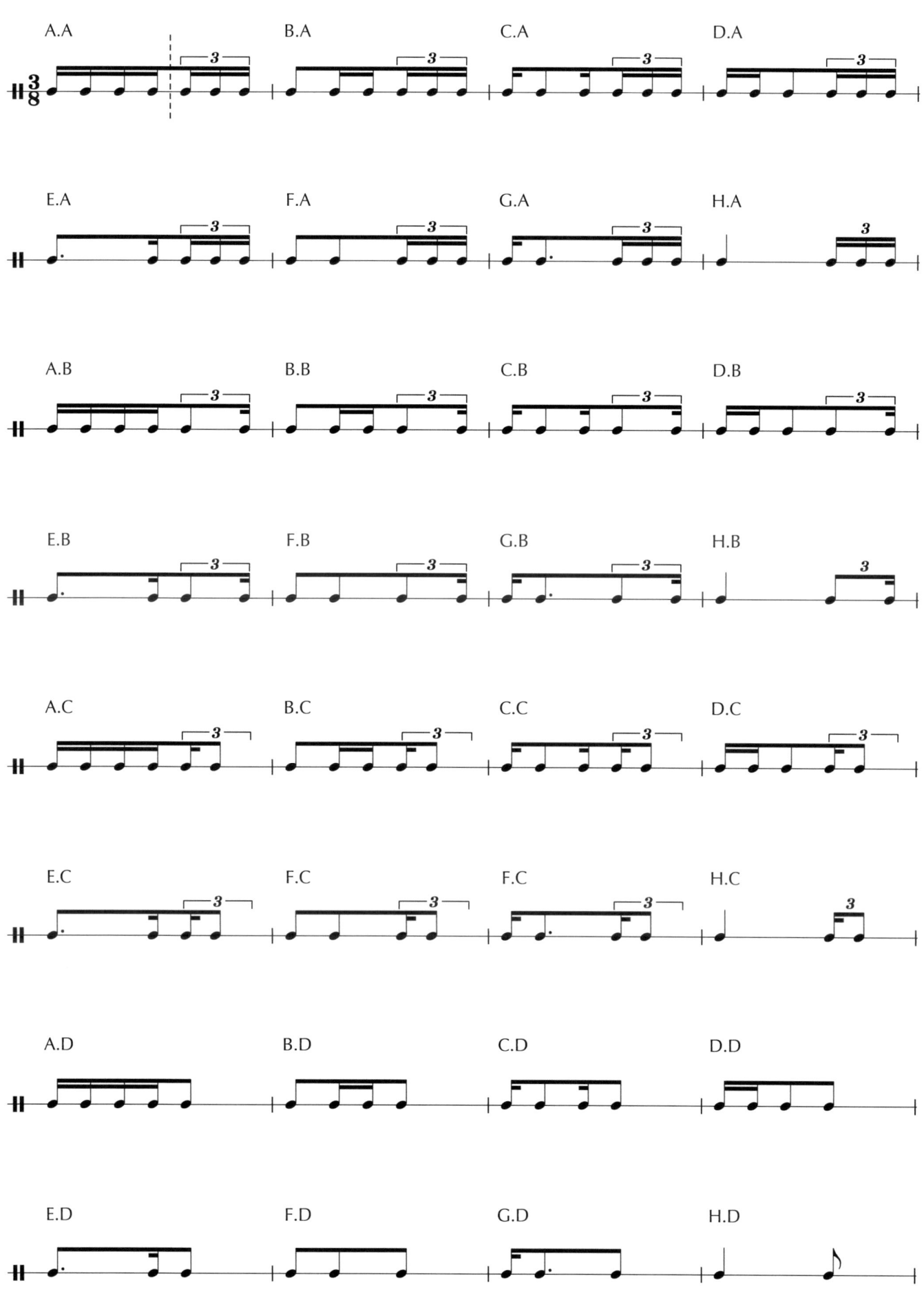

What you have learned

In chapter 7 you have:

- worked with combinations of triplets and even note values.

CHAPTER

Thirty-second notes

Thirty-second notes

In chapter 1 we looked at eight rhythms (A-H) built from four eighth notes. In chapter 2 you did the same thing based on four sixteenth notes. Now you will go to the next halving of notes which is thirty-second notes. In a bar of 4/4-time you will be able to fit thirty-two notes or rests of this value. To make it easier we will practice these rhythms in 2/8-time.

It's the same procedure as earlier. The rhythms are created by tying together two or more notes, thus creating eight possible rhythms. The names in this chapter are the same: A-H. They are merely a reference for you, just as in earlier chapters.

Thirty-second notes are more common in slower tempi where the pulse can be felt as eighth notes. But of course they exist in all kinds of tempi.

In Basic Exercise 8A we will use 2/8-time which will make it easier to manage these rhythms.

**BASIC EXERCISE
8A**

IMPORTANT EXERCISE

You can find all Basic Exercises with sound on our website:

www.khmp.se

**NOTE!
SEE EACH RHYTHM
AS A PICTURE!**

1. Start an **eighth note pulse** at 75-90 BPM.

2. Your teacher plays **rhythm A**. Student mimics.

3. Add one rhythm at a time until you have managed all of them (A-H).

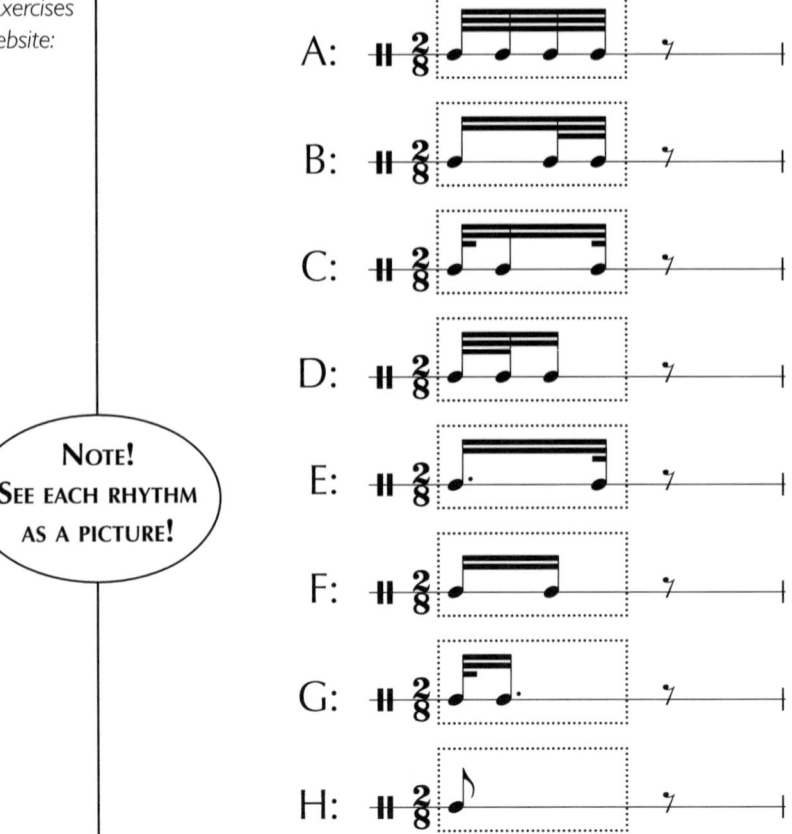

Note: On the next page these rhythms are beamed together which is common.

Exercise 8

A - No TIES (original)

❏ C - Ties between the rhythm-pictures within the bar

❏ E - Ties between the bars

❏ G - Ties according to both C and E

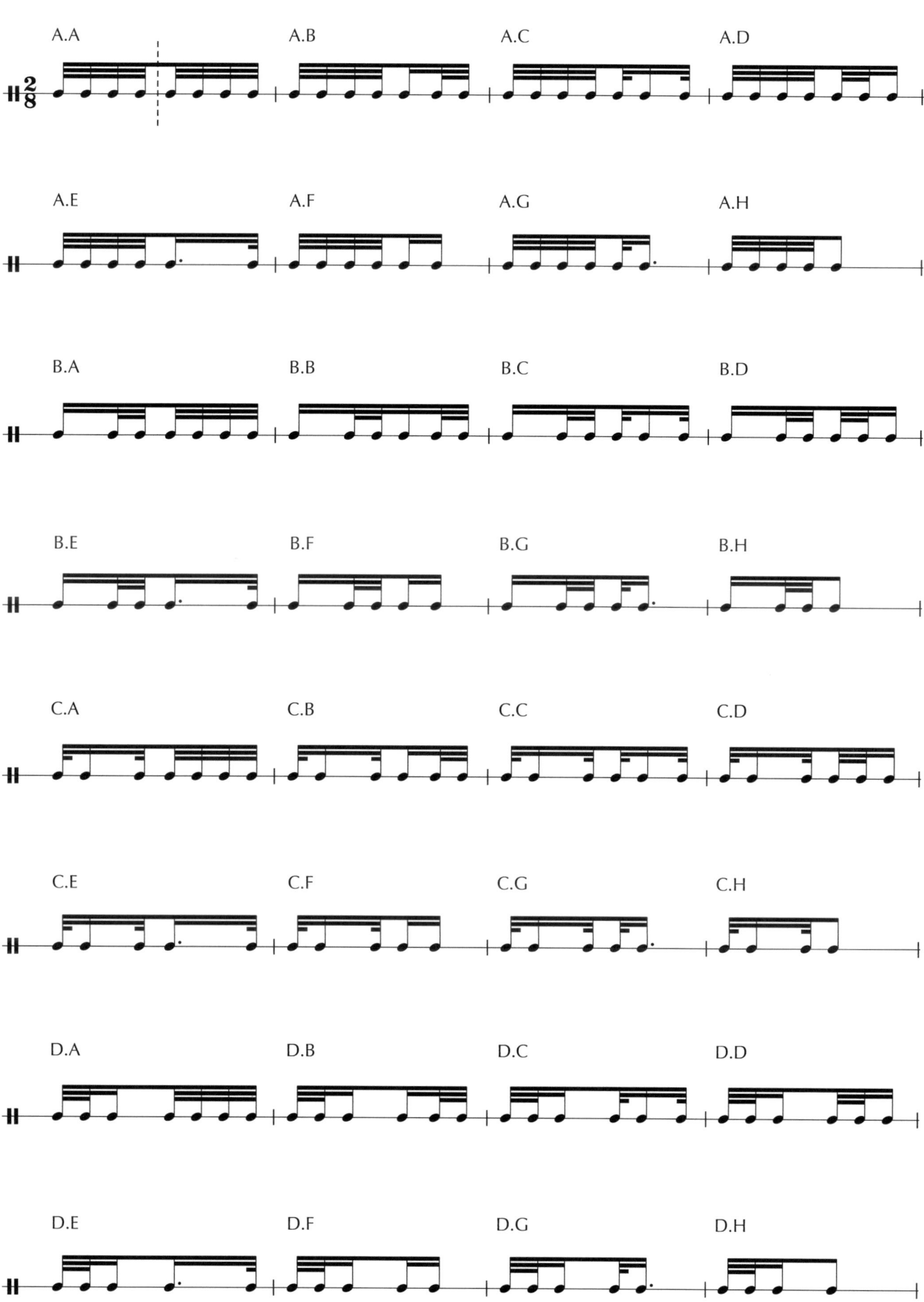

Exercise 8 cont.

A - No TIES (original)
- ❏ C - Ties between the rhythm-pictures within the bar
- ❏ E - Ties between the bars
- ❏ G - Ties according to both C and E

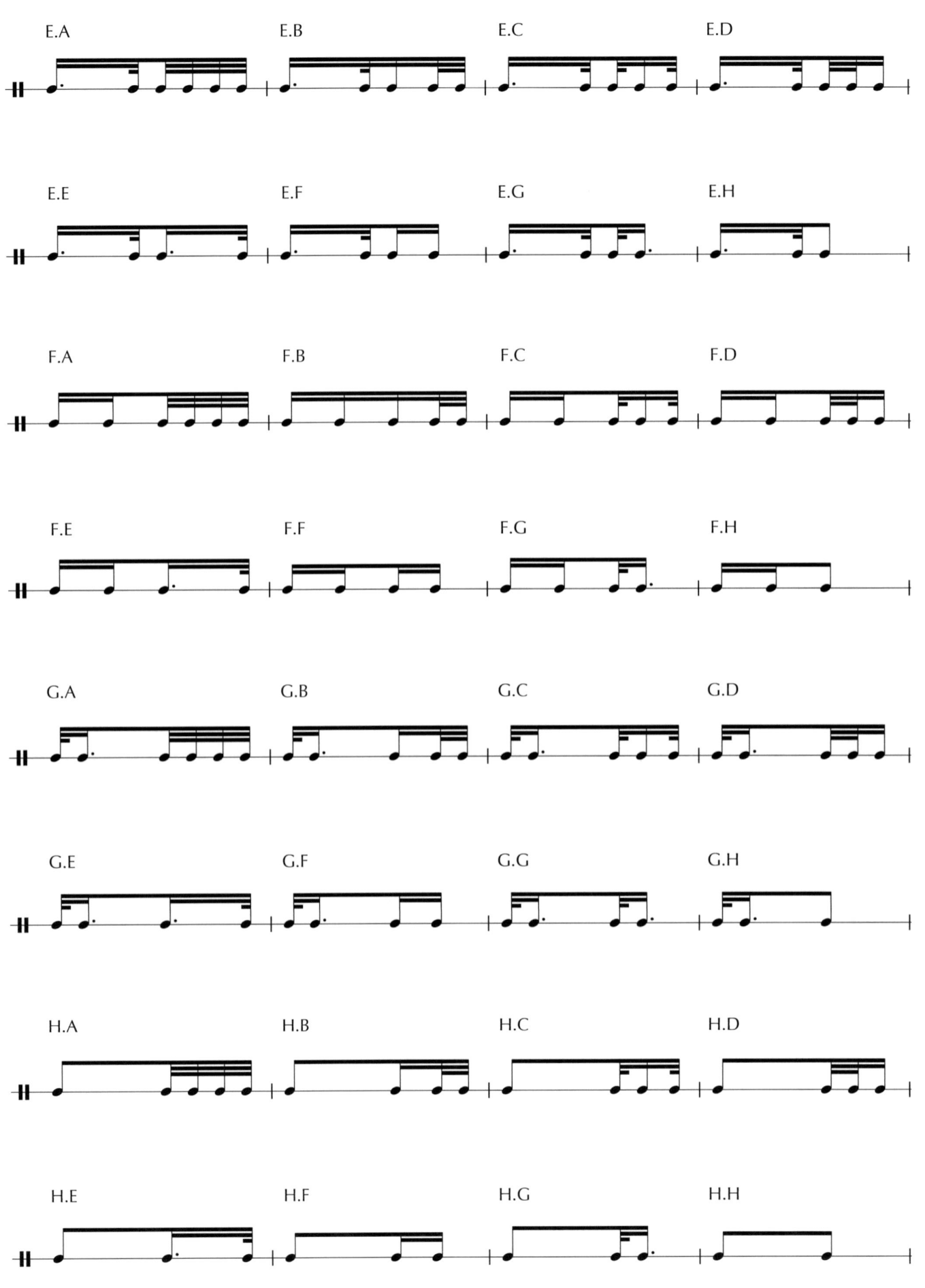

MAKE COPIES OF THIS PAGE!
Write TIES according to: C, E or G.
See page 139.

BASIC EXERCISE
8B
RESTS

IMPORTANT EXERCISE

You can find all Basic Exercises with sound on our website:

www.khmp.se

NOTE!
SEE EACH RHYTHM
AS A PICTURE!

Exercise 8a can be photocopied so that you can make your own exercises with ties! Before doing that, I think you should learn these eight rhythms with a rest in the beginning of each rhythm. Learn them in the same way as earlier. Your teacher plays/sings and you mimic while looking at the rhythm.
Eighth note pulse at 75-90 BPM:

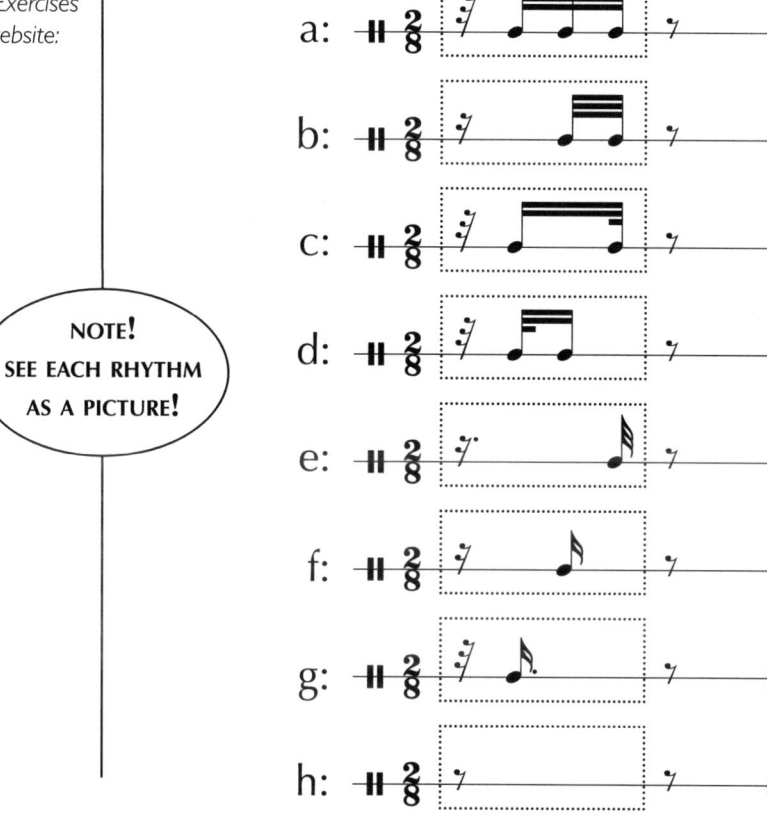

Make your own exercises

When you have finished Exercise 8b on the following pages, make three photocopies of Exercise 8a on pages 137-138 and write **ties** as follows:

- Write ties between the rhythm-pictures within the bar. (Var. C):

- Write ties between the bars. (Var. E):

- Write ties between both the rhythm-pictures within the bar AND between the bars. (Var. G):

Exercise 8b

Rhythms from Basic Exercise 8a and 8b.

Exercise 8b cont.

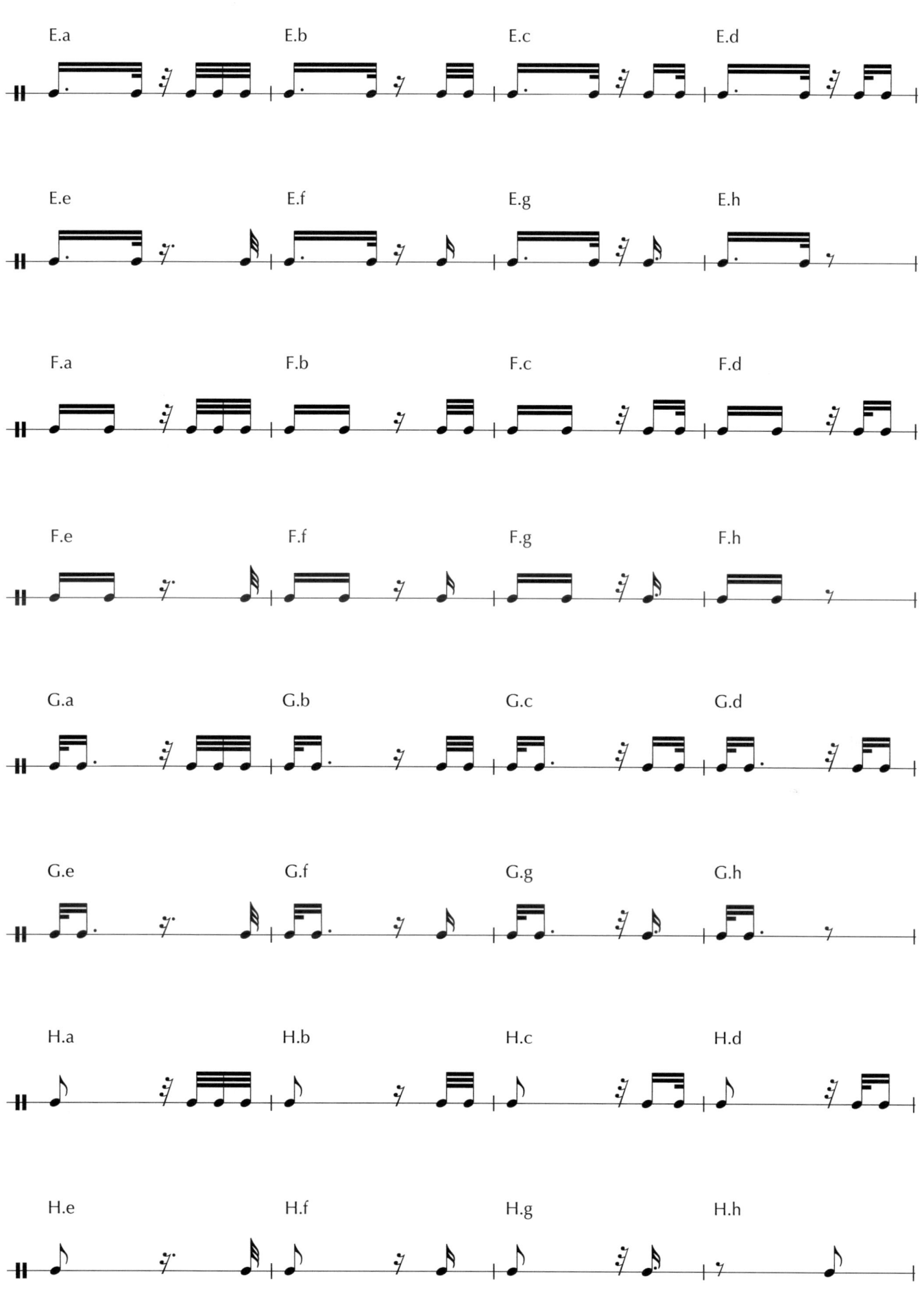

Thirty-second notes and other note values

Here are some short examples combining thirty-second notes and rhythms from earlier chapters.

You can choose to feel the pulse either as eighth notes or quarter notes. It is good to try both ways. (Eighth note pulse at 100 BPM and quarter note pulse at 50 BPM).

Exercise 8-2a

Rhythms from Basic Exercises 2a and 8a.

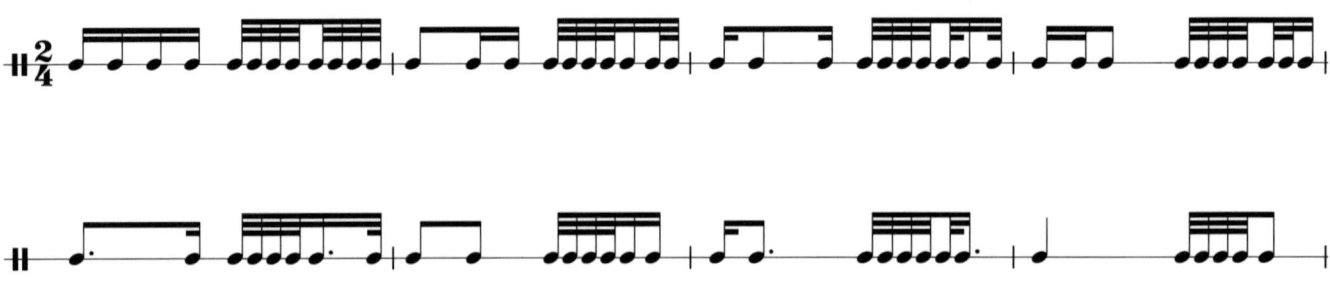

Exercise 8-3a

Rhythms from Basic Exercises 8a and 2a.

Thirty-second notes in combination with sixteenth note triplets

On the next page you will find rhythms from Basic Exercises 8a and 6a but also from Basic Exercises 8b and 6b (rests).

Exercise 8-4a

Rhythms from Basic Exercises 8a and 6a.

Exercise 8-4b

Rhythms from Basic Exercises 8a, 8b, 6a and 6b.

What you have learned

In chapter 8 we have worked with

- eight new rhythm-pictures created from four thirty-second notes.
  (Basic Exercise 8a).

- eight new rhythm-pictures with rests based on thirty-second notes
  (Basic Exercise 8b).

- combinations of rhythms from Basic Exercises 8a and 8b together with
  rhythms form earlier chapters.

Remember that it is very good to work in several chapters side by side. By following the study plan at the end of the book you will automatically do that.

CHAPTER

Eighth notes and 6/8-time

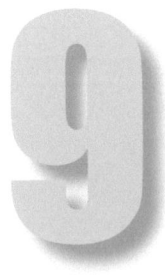

Eighth notes and 6/8-time

The rhythms we find in this chapter, that talks about 6/8-time, will remind you of the ones in chapter 5, where we worked with eighth note triplets.

In 6/8-time it is common to feel the pulse in two (beats per bar) instead of six. Both ways are common but usually you feel the pulse in two at higher tempi.

We will start to look at rhythms based on three eighth notes. Here we can create four rhythms, A-D.

Note how they remind of the rhythms in Basic Exercise 5a in chapter 5.

BASIC EXERCISE 9A

IMPORTANT EXERCISE

You can find all Basic Exercises with sound on our website:

www.khmp.se

1. Start an **eighth note pulse** at 180 BPM or a **dotted quarter note pulse** at 60 BPM.

2. Let your teacher play/sing **rhythm A**. Student mimics.

3. Learn one rhythm at a time until you have mastered all four (A-D).

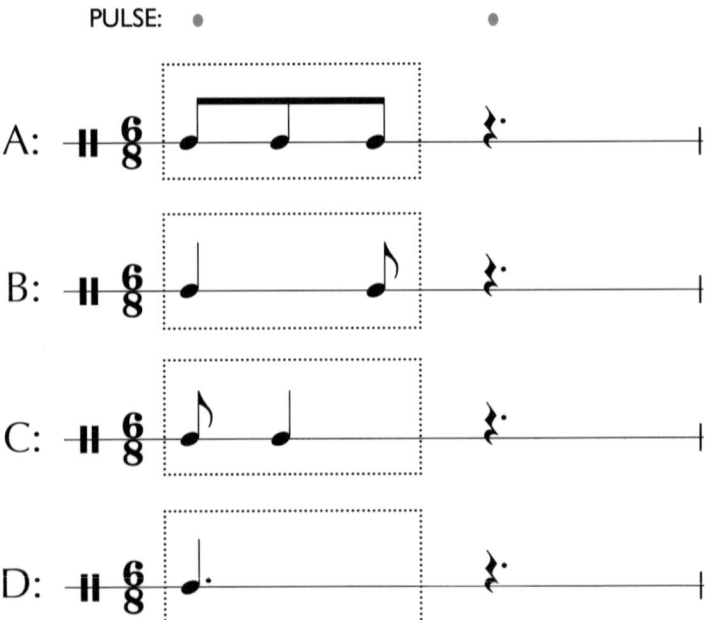

Note: Try to feel the pulse either in two beats per bar OR six beats per bar. That also goes for the following exercises.

> Remember to divide each bar into two parts and see each rhythm as a picture.

Exercise 9a
Rhythms from Basic Exercise 9a.

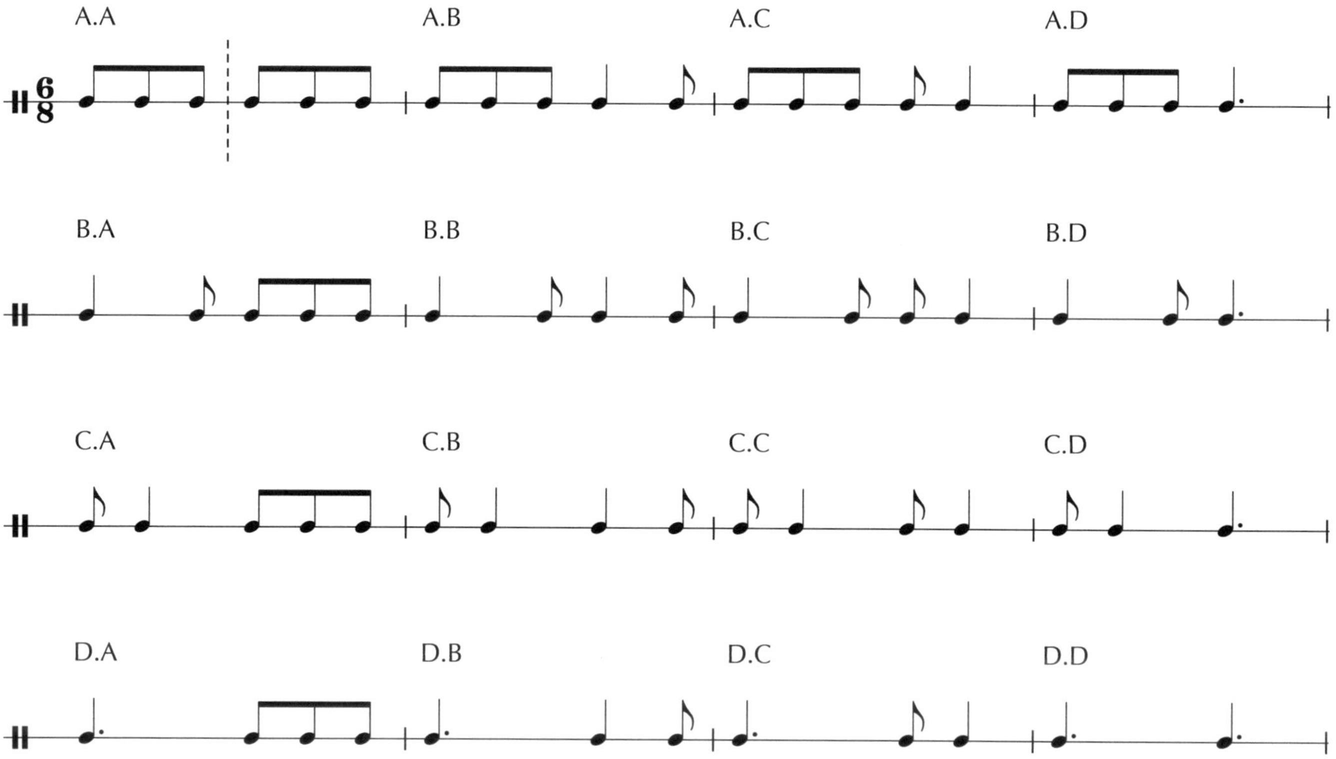

A.A   A.B   A.C   A.D

B.A   B.B   B.C   B.D

C.A   C.B   C.C   C.D

D.A   D.B   D.C   D.D

BASIC EXERCISE 9B

RESTS

IMPORTANT EXERCISE

You can find all Basic Exercises with sound on our website:

www.khmp.se

1. Start an **eighth note pulse** at 180 BPM or a **dotted quarter note pulse** at 60 BPM.

2. Your teacher plays/sings **rhythm a**. Student mimics.

3. Add one rhythm at a time until you have mastered all four (a-d).

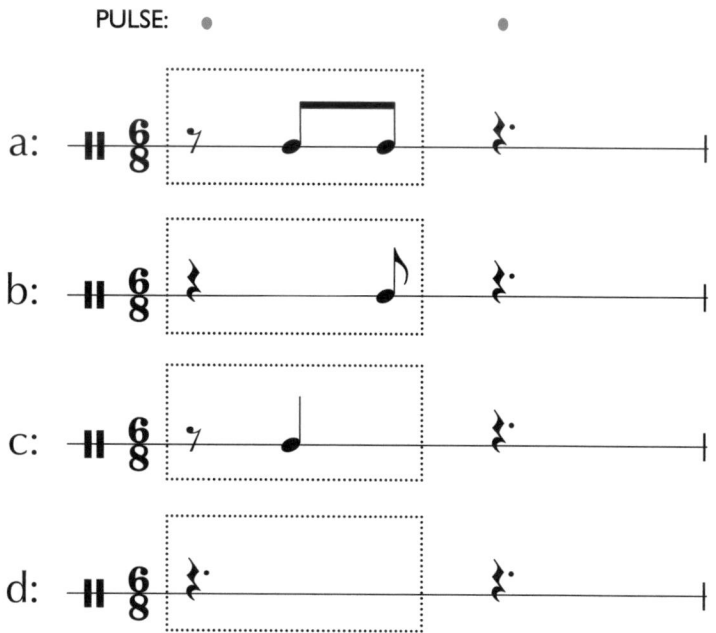

Remember to divide each bar into two parts and see each rhythm as a picture.

Exercise 9b

Rhythms from Basic Exercises 9a and 9b.

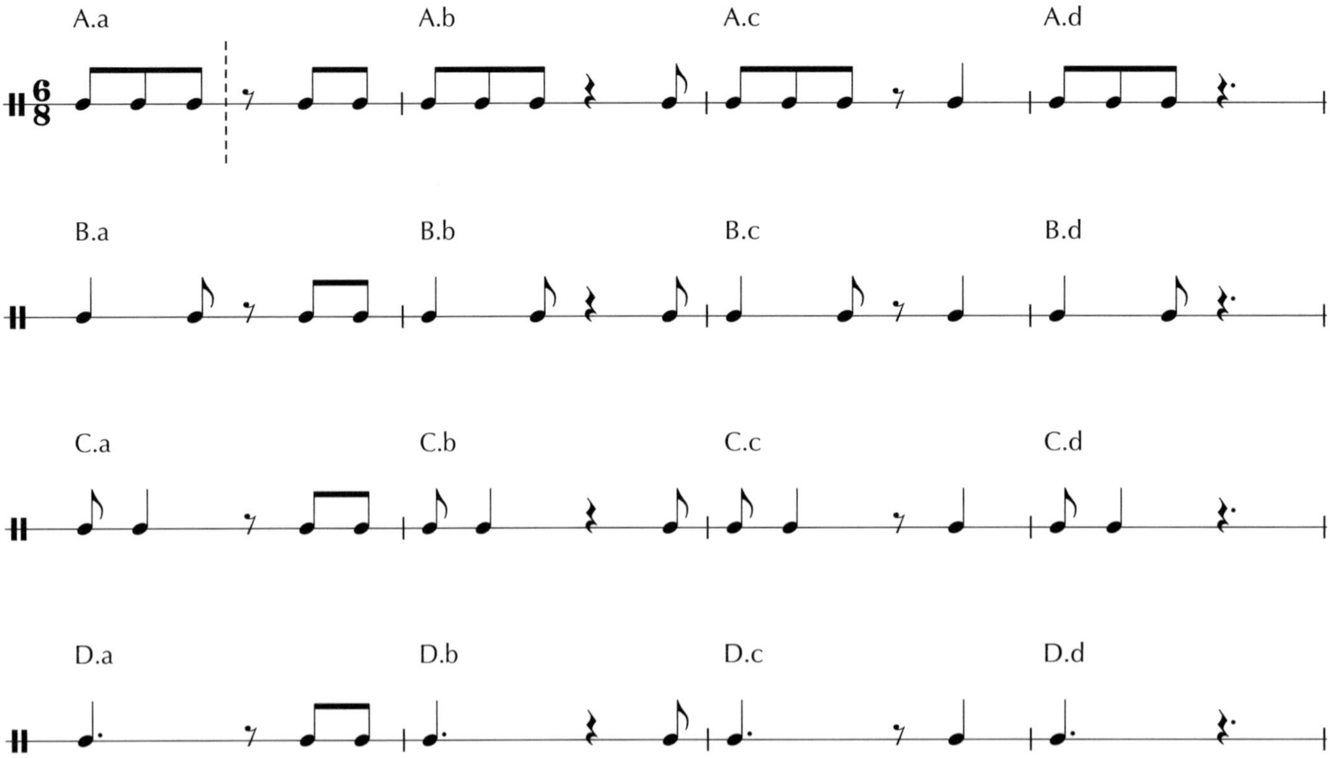

Exercise 9c

Same as 9b but with ties instead of rests..

or: 𝅗𝅥.

Exercise 9d

Rhythms from Basic Exercises 9b and 9a.

Exercise 9e

Same as 9d but with ties instead of rests..

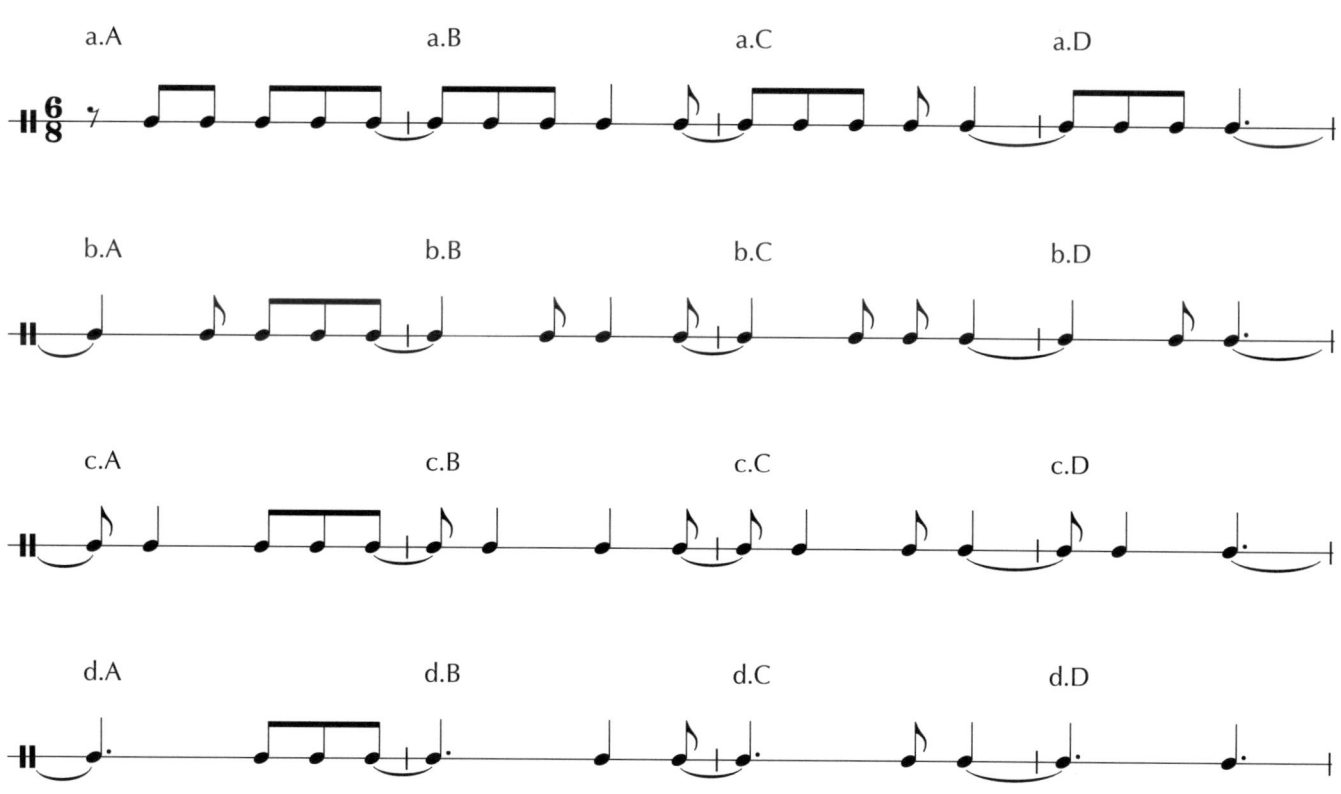

Exercise 9f

Rhythms from Basic Exercise 9b.

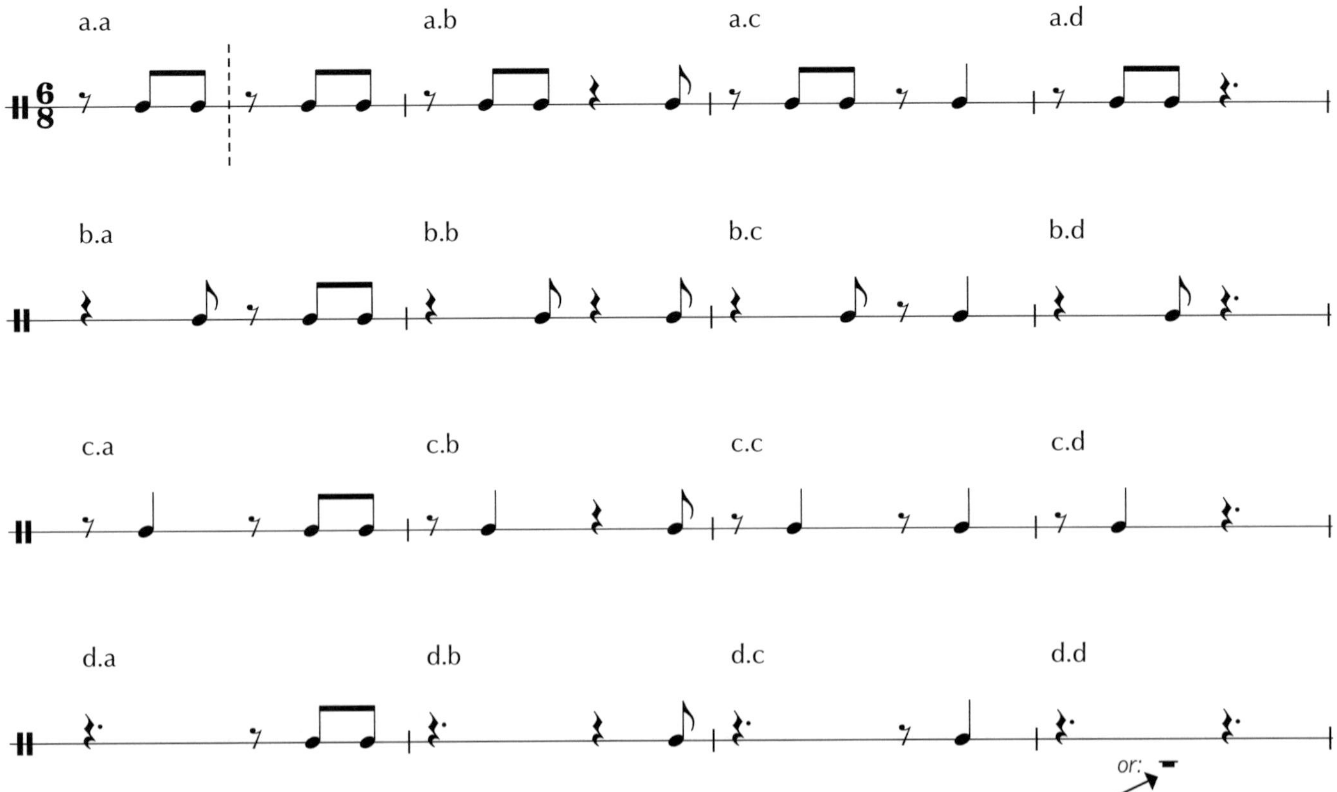

Whole rest. This rest indicates silence for a full bar, no matter what time signature it is.

Exercise 9g

Same as 9f but with ties instead of rests.

*** Rewritten to another note value, instead of using ties.*

CHAPTER 10

Sixteenth notes and 6/8-time

Sixteenth notes and 6/8-time

If we split a 6/8 bar in two, you will get three eighth note beats on each side. Let's fill these with sixteenth notes, which will give us six notes to work with. It looks like this:

Note that you can choose to beam/group the notes in different ways. They will still sound the same. Let's call any of the group of six notes above for **rhythm A**.

Since we now have six notes as a starting point, we will get many more combinations compared to earlier chapters, where we had only four or three notes as a starting point. We will get **thirty rhythms** in total derived from these six notes. It will obviously be much harder to learn them in the same way as we have done earlier in this book. Of course, you can do that but I will show you another way.

First, let's look at all the rhythms we can create from these six sixteenth notes. In the left columns below you can see how they are created by tying two or more notes together. **In the right columns** you see how the rhythms usually are written:

Note: *You have to use ties in a couple of rhythms to get all combinations!*

How can we remember all these rhythms?

Well, it is not easy but here is a tip that has helped me. It doesn't quite cover all thirty rhythms but most of them.

If you try to see the first four notes as rhythm A from Chapter 2 (sixteenth notes) and then just add another two sixteenth notes to that rhythm. Like this:

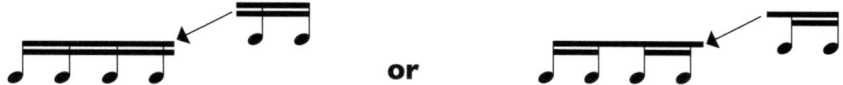

By doing this it can be easier to grasp all rhythms in this chapter. You can also look at the two added notes as rhythm F from chapter 8 (thirtysecond notes).

EXAMPLE 10-1

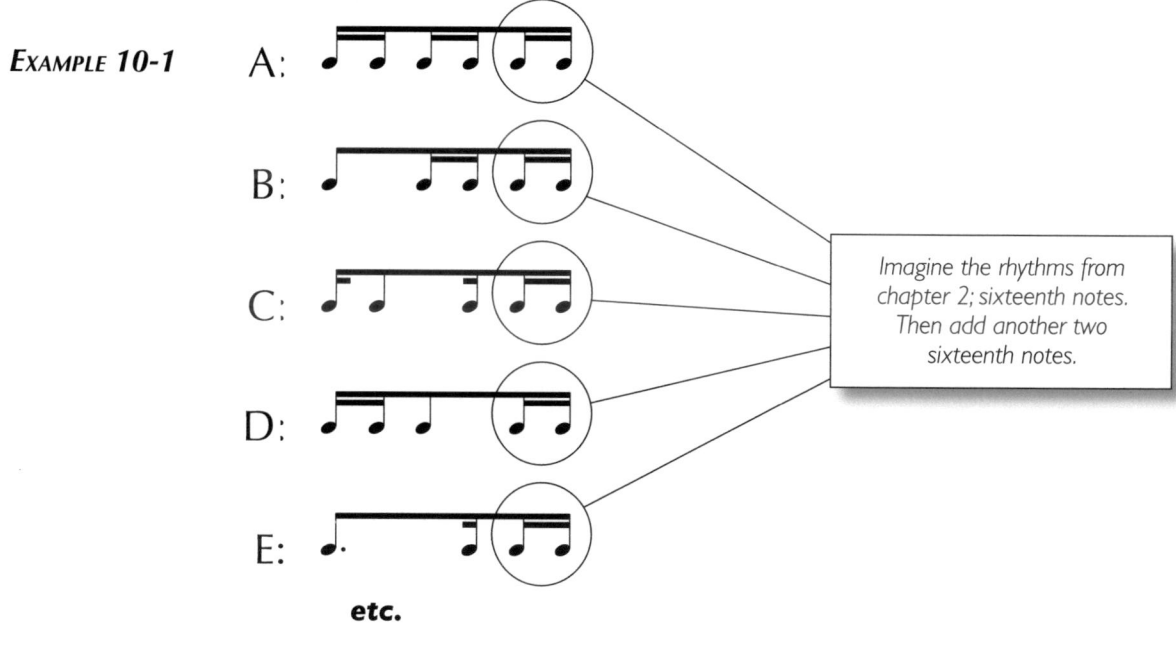

Imagine the rhythms from chapter 2; sixteenth notes. Then add another two sixteenth notes.

etc.

. . . .

EXAMPLE 10-2

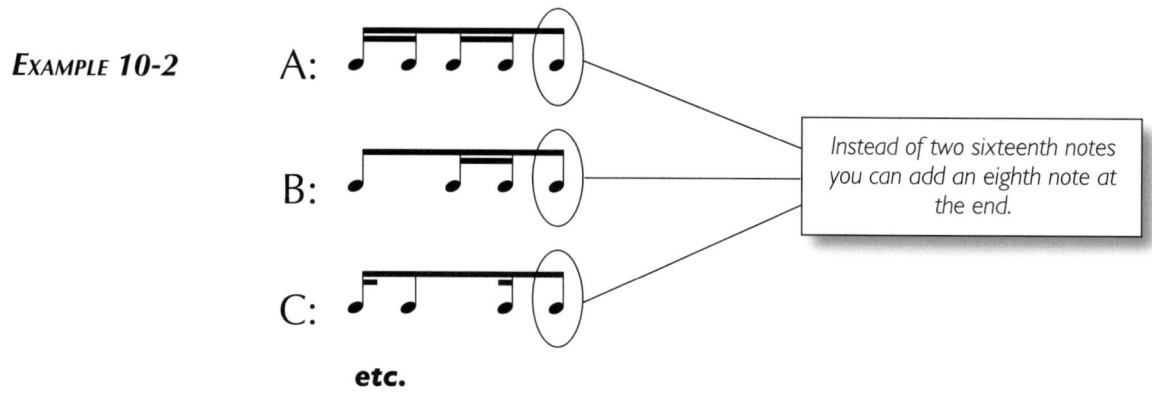

Instead of two sixteenth notes you can add an eighth note at the end.

etc.

EXAMPLE 10-3

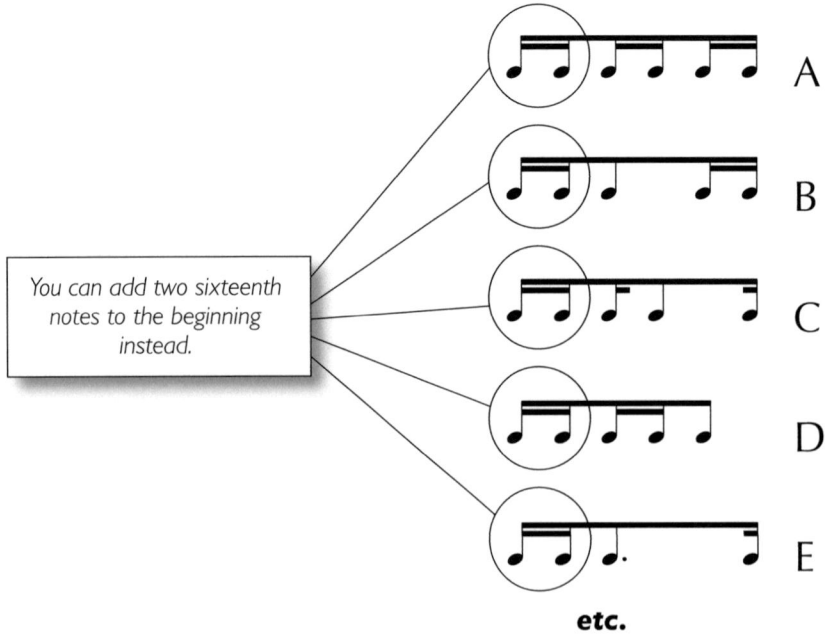

You can add two sixteenth notes to the beginning instead.

A
B
C
D
E

etc.

EXAMPLE 10-4

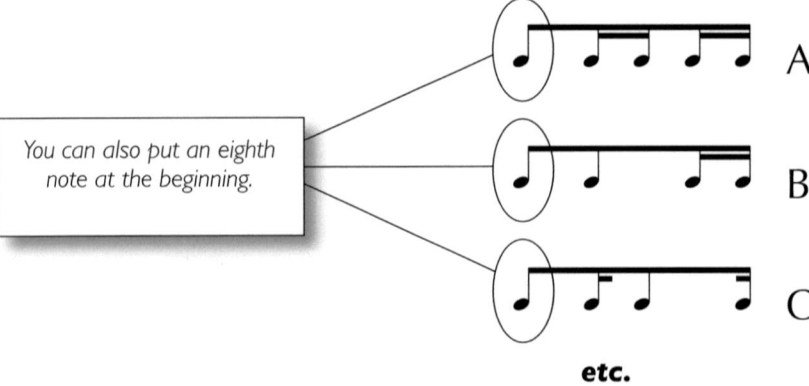

You can also put an eighth note at the beginning.

A
B
C

etc.

The rhythms from Ex. 10-1 – 10-4 above are presented in full on the next page in four Basic Exercises.

Note that the same rhythm can appear in several exercises and also be named differently. This is because you can view them from different perspectives.

The important thing now is to try to find the rhythms from chapter 2 (sixteenth notes) and then add one *eighth note beat* either in the beginning of the rhythm or at the end. In this way you are using your earlier skills to master these rhythms more easily.

Note: Basic Exercises 10-1 – 10-4 will not show all the rhythms. You can see all of them on page 152.

BASIC EXERCISE 10-1 *IMPORTANT EXERCISE*

See example 10-1
on page 153.

Pulse:
...or:

1A:
1B:
1C:
1D:
1E:
1F:
1G:
1H:

BASIC EXERCISE 10-2 *IMPORTANT EXERCISE*

See example 10-2
on page 153.

Pulse:
...or:

2A:
2B:
2C:
2D:
2E:
2F:
2G:
2H:

BASIC EXERCISE 10-3 *IMPORTANT EXERCISE*

See example 10-3
on page 154.

Pulse:
...or:

3A:
3B:
3C:
3D:
3E:
3F:
3G:
3H:

BASIC EXERCISE 10-4 *IMPORTANT EXERCISE*

See example 10-4
on page 154.

Pulse:
...or:

4A:
4B:
4C:
4D:
4E:
4F:
4G:
4H:

When you have spent some time with the rhythms on the previous page you can move on to the exercises below.

Since there are a great number of rhythms and combinations, we will only be able to cover a few in this book.

The most important thing is that you practice these rhythms so you get a feel for 6/8-time and rhythms covering three eighth note beats. It is impossible to prepare yourself for all imaginable rhythms that will come in front of you, but by spending time with written music you will come across more complex rhythms and with experience it will be easier and easier to figure them out.

Here are a few examples based on the rhythms from last page:

Exercise 10-1a

Exercise 10-2a

Exercise 10-3a

Exercise 10-4a

On the next page you will find rhythms with rests, just like earlier in the book, where the first note is replaced with a corresponding rest.

You will not find another *Basic Exercise* to present this. Instead you'll have to figure this out by yourself or with your teacher.
After that there are some exercises with ties.

Exercise 10-1b

Exercise 10-2b

Exercise 10-3b

Exercise 10-4b

Exercise 10-1c

Exercise 10-2c

Exercise 10-3c

Exercise 10-4c

Exercise 10-1d

Exercise 10-2d

Exercise 10-3d

Exercise 10-4d

Exercise 10-1e

Exercise 10-2e

Exercise 10-3e

Exercise 10-4e

Exercise 10-1g

Exercise 10-2g

Exercise 10-3g

Exercise 10-4g

. . . .

Combinations with other note values

Each group of two sixteenth notes below can be replaced by rhythms based on **sixteenth note triplets**[1] or **thirty-second notes**[2].

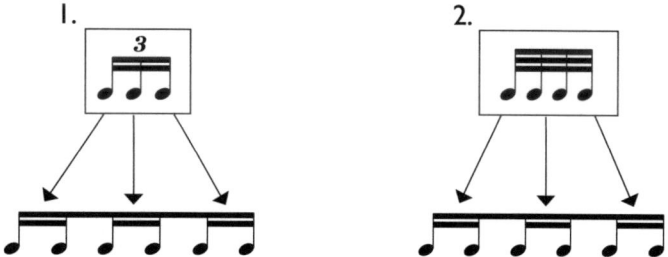

If we put four thirty-second notes in the first group of sixteenth notes it will look like this:

On the next page there are some exercises where you can practice this.

Exercise 10-5

Exercise 10-6

Exercise 10-7

Exercise 10-8

Exercise 10-9

Exercise 10-10

Exercise 10-11

Exercise 10-12

What you have learned

In chapter 10 you have:

- worked with rhythms based on six sixteenth notes in 6/8-time.

- realized that there are thirty rhythms to keep track of if you want to learn all the combinations of these six sixteenth notes.

- used a shortcut to master most of these thirty rhythms by using rhythms from chapter 2 (sixteenth notes) and then adding two sixteenth notes or an eighth note before or after the rhythms from chapter 2.

- worked with combinations of ties and rests in these thirty rhythms.

- replaced one group of two sixteenth notes (one beat) with rhythms from chapter 8 (thirty-second notes) or from chapter 6 (sixteenth note triplets).

CHAPTER

Time signatures

Time signatures

A **bar** is constructed with a number of **beats** where the first beat is accentuated. For instance; 2 beats, 3 beats, 4 beats 5 beats 6 beats, 7 beats etc. The number of beats in a bar indicates the **time signature**. In modern Western music this is written as **fractions:**

$$\frac{3}{4} \qquad \frac{6}{8}$$

The **upper number** indicates the **number of beats** per bar and the **lower number** indicates **what kind of beat** it is; *quarter notes, eighth notes, half notes etc.*

You can also find a couple of symbols replacing fractions, like: **C** or **¢**

These symbols come from older music notations and have survived the test of time.

C equals nowadays 4/4-time and is originally a **half circle** (not the letter C), indicating **tempus imperfectum** (imperfect time) which originally was some kind of 2-time or 6-time. It is sometimes referred to as **common time**, but that is actually a modern interpretation.

O A full circle on the other hand (no longer in use) symbolized **perfect time** which was 3-time or 9-time, *the divine time signature.* (The famous mathematician Pythagoras is said to have considered the sphere a divine geometric figure, hence the circle).

¢ is a half circle with a vertical line through it and is still in use, and indicates that the **pulse is half notes** in 4/4-time. (Or more accurately; 2/2-time.) It is also referred to as **cut time** or **alla breve**. *In this book you can try* **cut time** *if you play all 4/4-time examples with a half note pulse instead.*

> *The big question is how we can improve our reading when it comes to different time signatures. Personally, I prefer to view rhythms in different time signatures as rhythm-pictures based on rhythms from 4/4-time or 6/8-time. More on this later.*

There's tons of information about time signatures online and you have hours of reading if you wish. In this book we focus on the actual reading of rhythms, not theory, so I won't go into this any deeper.

On the next page you will find different time signatures. Some of them you may never encounter and others are more common, depending on what kind of music you usually play/sing.

An accent over a note is marked by a > and a – indicates a softer accent.

Different time signatures

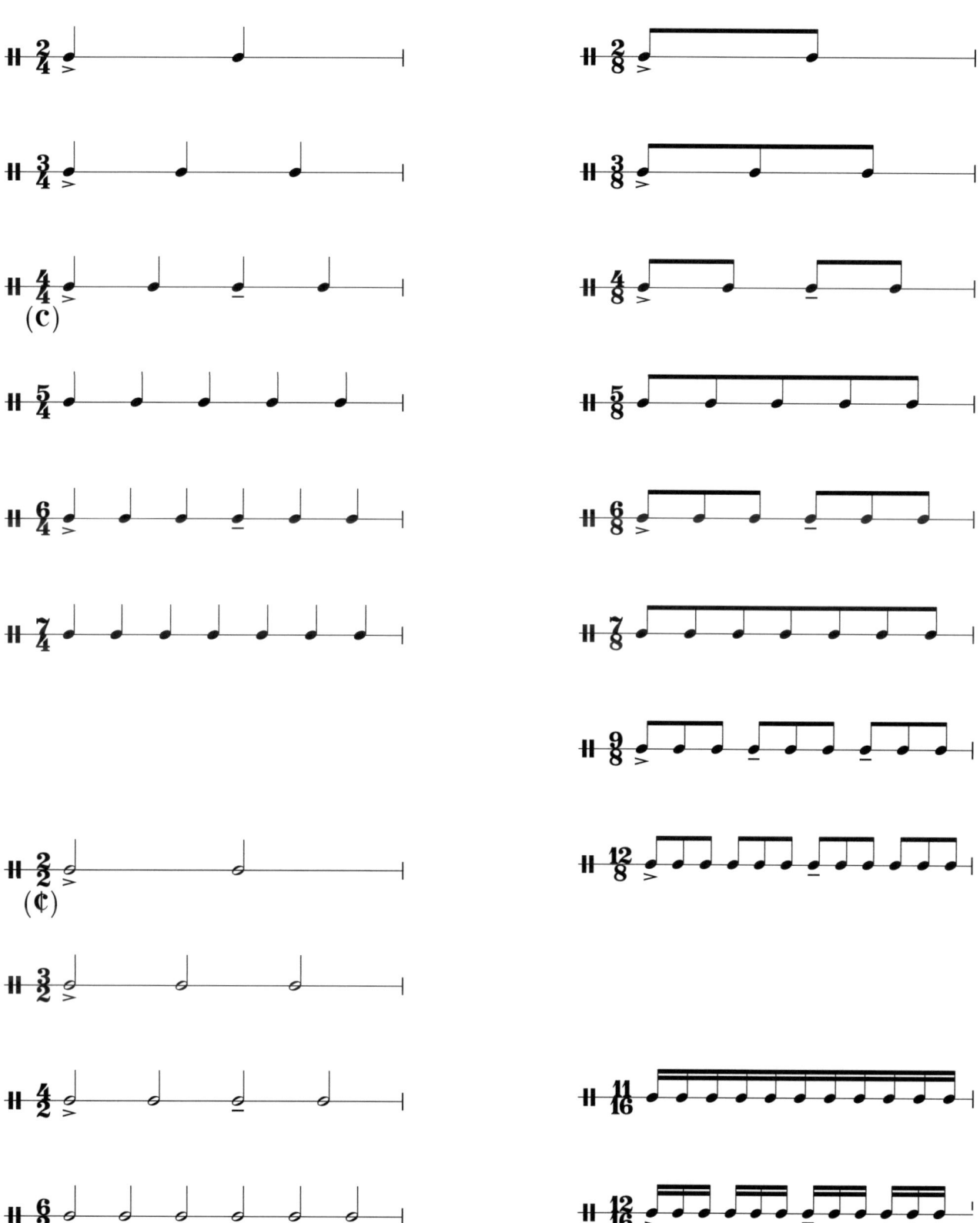

There are even more time signatures to explore and one time signature I'd like to mention is 1/2-time or 1/4-time. They appear mostly in marching music since they automatically indicate accents on every beat. The reason you want to avoid 2/4-time in marching music is because the beats in 2/4-time are *accented-unaccented* which could cause the marching band to stagger.

Odd time

When talking about time signatures you can sometimes hear the expression **odd time**. So what is meant by that? Does it mean there is an odd number in the time signature? Or does it mean it is an *unusual* time signature? Well, neither is true!

Let's look at 3/4-time as an example. 3/4-time has an odd number (3) in its time signature but is still not an odd time signature in the correct sense. And 3/4-time is also very common. So, what is an odd time signature? Perhaps that expression is not the best one. What *odd time* actually refers to is *time signatures that **can't be divided by 2 or 3**, like 5/4, 7/8, and 11/8 etc.*

So how do we approach odd time when it comes to reading music? Well, there are some tricks that you can use.

First, let's remind ourselves about the way we read and play 6/8-time. In 6/8 you can either feel the beat in 6 beats or 2 beats (and sometimes in 3 beats). Perhaps 2 beats (two dotted quarter notes) is the most common:

In 4/4-time you can also feel the pulse in two (half-notes), at least in faster tempi. And in 3/4-time you can feel the pulse as one beat per bar (dotted half note).

In odd time you can combine different ways of feeling the pulse. For instance, in 5/8-time you can feel the pulse as a **dotted quarter note** (just as in 6/8-time) plus **one quarter note** (one beat in 4/4-time):

In 7/8-time you can have the pulse as **a quarter note + a quarter note + a dotted quarter note,** or any variation thereof:

How to feel the pulse depends on how the music is composed and hopefully you can feel this when reading/playing.

Below you find some examples of how to divide the pulse in some odd time signatures with an eighth note pulse.

Split the bar into two or three sections (or more) so that you can *sort out three eighth notes as one beat = a dotted quarter-note*, thus using the 6/8-time-feel on those beats. The other beats are quarter notes from for instance 4/4-time:

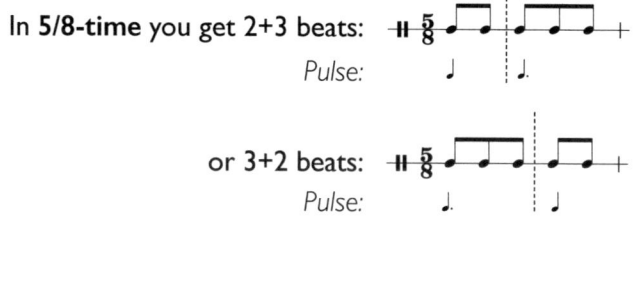

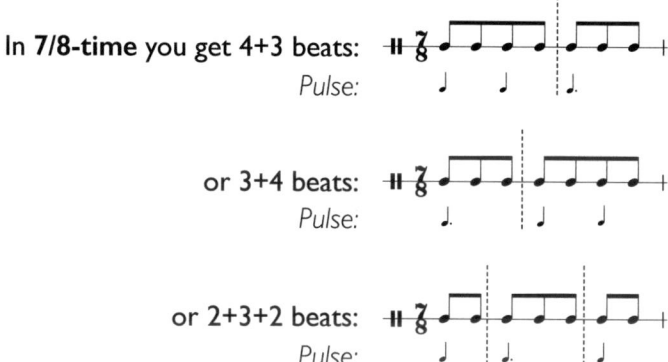

Conclusion:
In odd time you often find rhythm-pictures from both **6/8-time** (or 3/8-time) and from **4/4-time** (or 2/4-time).

5/8-time

Here are some examples in 5/8-time. Try to see two rhythm-pictures per bar, either as 2+3 or 3+2. (See previous page). You will see rhythm-pictures found in 6/8-time and 2/4-time (4/4-time). Instead of feeling the pulse as five beats try to feel it as two beats where one of them is a **dotted quarter note** and the other a **quarter note**. The music will guide you.

In the examples you will find rhythms from many chapters in the book.

Exercise 11-1

Exercise 11-2

Exercise 11-3

Exercise 11-4

Exercise 11-5

Exercise 11-6

Exercise 11-7

Exercise 11-8

Exercise 11-9

Exercise 11-10

7/8-time

Here are some examples in 7/8-time. You will find rhythm-pictures in 2/4-time, 4/4-time and 6/8-time from earlier chapters in the book.

Remember to divide the pulse in **dotted quarter notes** and **quarter notes** according to how the music is written.

Exercise 11-11

Exercise 11-12

Exercise 11-13

Whole rest.
This rest indicates silence for a full bar,
no matter what time signature it is.

Exercise 11-14

Exercise 11-15

Exercise 11-16

Mixed time signatures

In some music you will find changes of time signatures. Like going from 3/4-time to 4/4-time in the middle of the piece. In most sheet music you can also find notations about tempo changes, style, performance notes etc, which is not covered in this book.

In the following example you can see different time signatures in the same piece of music. It also starts with a **pick-up bar**. (You will learn more about pick-up bars in the next chapter).

Try to find the places where you move to **dotted quarter note** pulse!

Exercise 11-17

What you have learned

In chapter 11 you have:

- worked with different time signatures.

- looked at ways of handling odd time. (5/8, 7/8)

- worked with mixed time signatures

- learned how to use different types of pulse-values.

CHAPTER 12

Pick-up bars

Pick-up bars

A musical phrase written before the first full bar in a musical piece is called a **pick-up bar** or **anacrusis**. It could be anything between a short note to an entire bar.

When the band leader or conductor starts off the music it is important to see the pick-up bar correctly. Sometimes when in a hurry you could easily misread the pick-up bar.

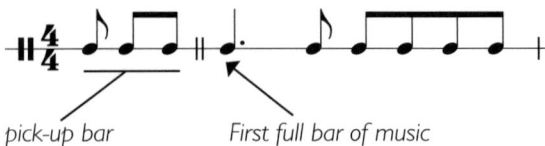

pick-up bar   *First full bar of music*

Let's take a look at some pick-up bars of different lengths. I have written a count off in grey as a guide but a conductor would usually just show the beat preceding the pick-up notes. The music written before the double bar line is the pick-up bar. *Note that there is not always a double bar line indicating this.*

Another way of writing a pick-up bar is to add **a rest** before the first note(s) to make it easier to read and understand the length of the pick-up. Usually to get a **full beat** or a **full bar**. *Compare examples 12-13 and 12-15 below.*

Ex. 12-9

Ex. 12-10

Ex. 12-11

Ex. 12-12

Ex. 12-13

Here are some more examples:

Ex. 12-14

Ex. 12-15

Ex. 12-16

Ex. 12-17

Here are some pick-up bars in different time signatures:

Ex. 12-18

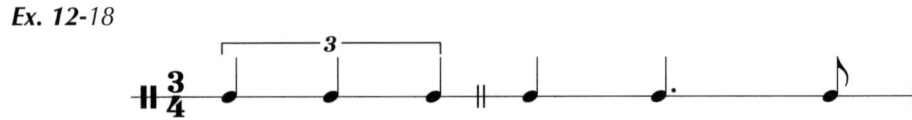

Ex. 12-19

Ex. 12-20

Ex. 12-21

Ex. 12-22

The pick-up bar is not always followed by a double bar line.

Ex. 12-23

A repeat sign can be the first bar line.

CHAPTER 13

Paraphrases and more

Paraphrases

When reading music, I often encounter variants or paraphrases of the rhythms that we have worked with in this book. Mostly I can recognize many of them instantly but sometimes I have to stop and really think what they mean. Often it is just a note made shorter with a rest added or a different beaming.

Talking about beams. In older printings of **vocal music**, beams are often only used when several notes are to be sung on one syllable, so called **melismatic singing**. We still have that in hymnals in churches here in Sweden.

Which do you think is easier to read, beams or flags?

flags instead of beams   *beams*

Let's look at some common paraphrases of the rhythms from Basic Exercise 1A in chapter 1:

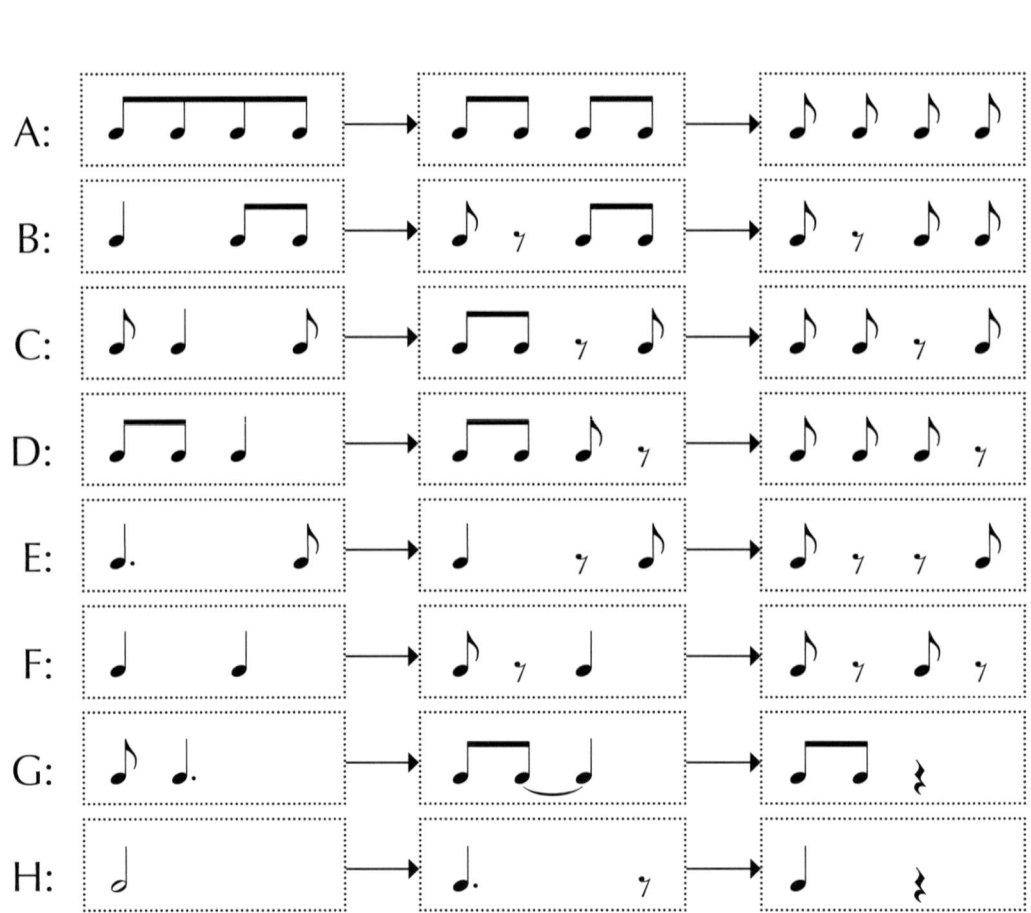

Here are some paraphrases of Basic Exercise 2A in chapter 2:

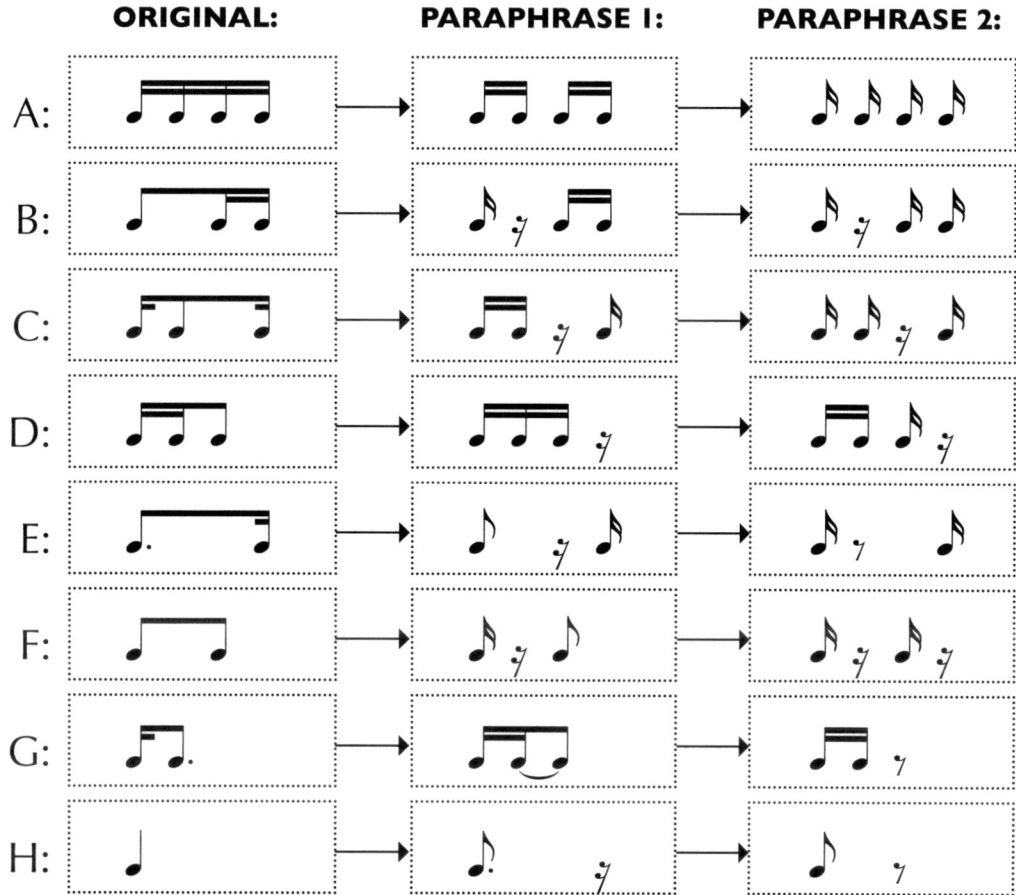

Here is a common paraphrase of **rhythm d** from Basic Exercise 2B:

original = *paraphrase*

Lazy rhythms

Laziness is the father of inventions, they say. Here is a common "lazy" rhythm:

"Lazy rhythm":

Original:

Note how you save one note, two flags, one stem and one tie with this *lazy rhythm*. Some arrangers/composers prefer them since they avoid ties and are faster to write. *Sure, ties can be confusing sometimes but I still prefer the notation used in this book. But be prepared to meet these lazy rhythms!*

We won't present any more paraphrases here but there are of course many more to explore. Just remember that you most certainly will have to figure some out in the future when reading music. That is why it is also good to have a *mathematical understanding* of the way rhythms are constructed. *(See Appendix!)*

So far, we have tried to see rhythms as a whole, or as *"words"* or *"pictures"* instead of *"single letters"*. But what happens when you, in normal text like this, encounter a word that you don't know? Like **brgwetyiosjhlzx**! Well, you have to break it down in to smaller segments, maybe even *"letter by letter"*! This is also true with written music. Both rhythms and pitches.

Perhaps you remember that I mentioned earlier to avoid sounding rhythms in a certain pattern, like: *1-e-an-a, 2-e-an-a, etc.* Although we *did* use a system like that in chapter 5, when learning triplets. Sometimes we have to use that kind of tool to sort out difficult rhythms. I have deliberately avoided a mathematical view of rhythms in this book since we are trying to develop our sight-reading technique using a more practical approach. And I believe this is the correct way of doing that. Still, I encourage you to get hold of a good music theory book for a more in-depth view of music. There you will also find other elements and expressions in written music not covered in this book that you need to know when sight-reading.

Articulation signs

There are some **articulation signs** used in writing music that can help you clean up the music. They are used instead of shortening a note value and adding rests. Here are four common ones that are used to sometimes shorten note values without having to use rests. The top row shows the notes with articulations and the bottom row shows how they are actually performed.

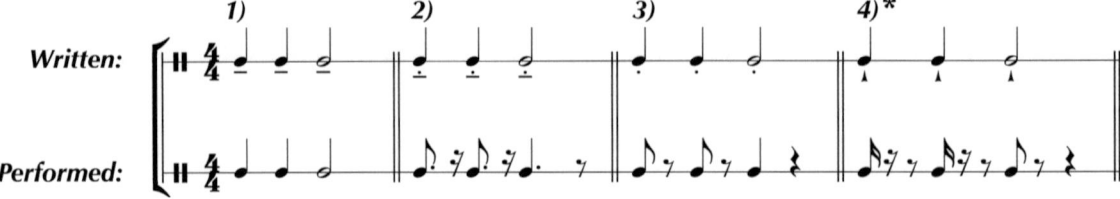

1) **Tenuto – Tied together** *Indicates that musical notes are played or sung smoothly and connected. That is, the player makes a transition from note to note with no silence in between.*

2) **Mezzo Staccato – Between long and short** *This is almost the normal way of playing notes when there are no signs attached to the them. Not too short not too long.*

3) **Staccato – Short note** *This indicates that the musician should play the note shorter than notated, usually half the value; the rest of the metric value is then silent. Staccato marks may appear on notes of any value, shortening their performed duration.*

4) **Staccatissimo – Very short note** *Indicates a longer silence after the note (as described above), making the note very short.*
    * Usually applied to quarter notes or shorter.

Note how much easier it is to read the top row! Use these signs to clean up your written music, making it easier for musicians to read.

Double dots

Before we look at **double dots**, we should take a look at dots in general. You encountered a dotted note in your first exercise (Basic Exercise 1A) but we didn't give it any theoretical attention at that point. We haven't been very theoretical at all I must say, and that is on purpose. But now it is time!

"A dot lengthens a note by half its value" is a phrase I learned when I started to learn how to read music. And if you know the theory about notes and how they are structured it is spot on. But what does it really mean?

Let's look at a dotted half note:

If we remove the dot, we get a half note:

What is its value? Meaning; how many beats, or subdivisions of a beat does a half note consist of? Two beats (two quarter notes) is the correct answer. *And what is the half of two beats (two quarter notes)?*

Yes, one beat (one quarter note):

So, a dotted half note equals **one half note + one quarter note** (2 + 1 beats):

If we take a dotted quarter note as an example:

Remove the dot and you end up with a quarter note:

What is its value/length? Yes, one beat (one quarter note).

What is the half of one quarter note? Yes, one eighth note:

Double dots

If we add another dot after the first dot of a quarter note you get a **double dotted quarter note:**

The second dot lengthens the note by one half of the first dot. In this case one sixteenth note:

A double dotted note is followed by a note or rest filling up what is missing mathematically to get a beat or several beats:

| one beat | two beats | four beats |

*Note: You can even find **tripple dots** in some music!*
Unfortunately, there are no exercises with double dots (or tripple dots) in this book.

What you have learned

In chapter 13 you have:

- seen that some rhythms can be written in different ways (paraphrases),.

- seen that it is good to also have a mathematical understanding of rhythms.

- seen the benefit of using articulation signs (tenuto, staccato, etc).

- taken a closer look on dotted notes and double dotted notes.

CHAPTER 14

Tips for keyboards, drums and ear training classes

Tips for Keyboards

Here are some tips on how to use the information in this book and take it to an extra level.

A trained eye might have noticed that the spacing between notes in this book sometimes look a bit wider than normal. This is on purpose. It is for helping keyboard players and others that need to practice reading **several systems at once**.

As a keyboard player you must also be able to see the music vertically – two systems at once (three if you play the church organ). The exercises in this book were designed for this purpose as an extra bonus!

There are two levels of difficulty in the following tip:

Level I

Use the exercises in this book but play two system at once. Level I is a little easier than Level 2. In Level I you play row I and 2 simultaneously. The right hand plays the upper system and the left hand plays the lower system. When changing row you must jump to row 3 and 4, as you would in a real situation. And after that to row 5 and 6 etc. This means that you will often get the same rhythm in both hands at the beginning of the bars = easier.

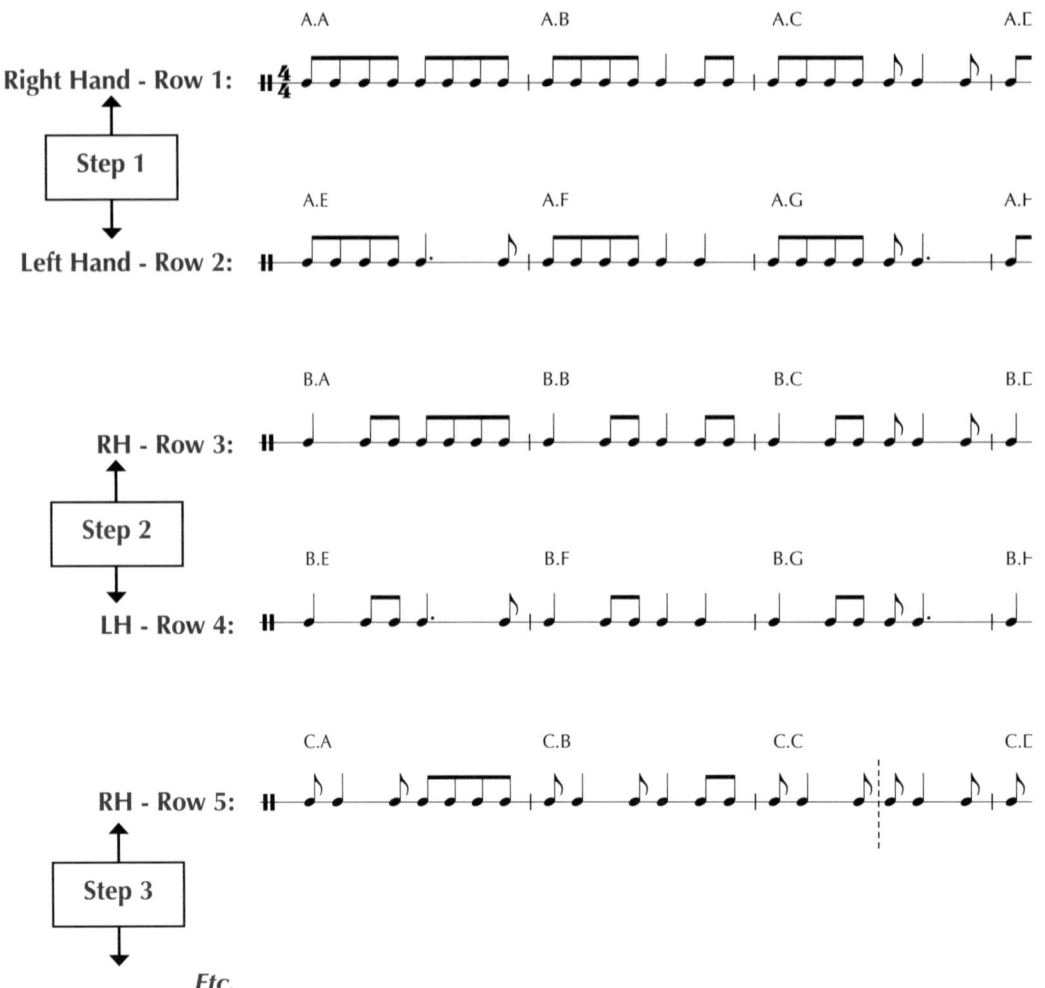

Level 2

A somewhat harder variation is to jump only one row down when changing systems. After playing row 1 and 2 you go to row 2 and 3, then to 3 and 4 etc. The combinations that arise (on every other step) are a little more difficult.

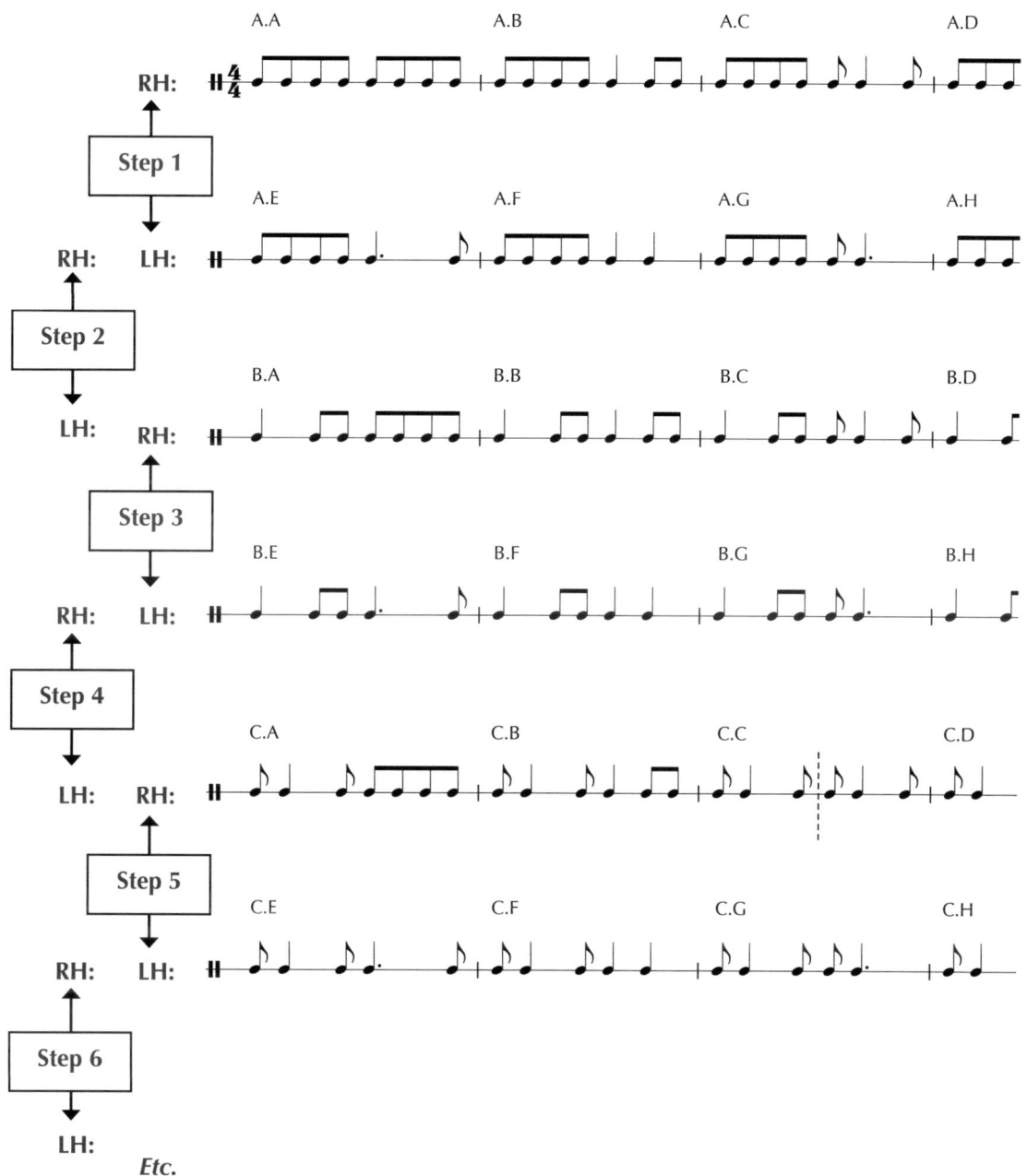

TIP: Use your fingers (1-5) to play the rhythms. Then it will be easier to play faster note values. You can play on your instrument (any pitches) or play with your fingers on a table.

Tips for Ear training classes

All exercises in this book can be done in group sessions, in ear training classes for instance. Here are some examples on how to work in groups:

1. **Half a bar each:**
    Split the class in two halves. First group plays/sings/claps the first half of every bar and the second group the second half. Switch! *(You can vary the sound between the groups by letting one group slap their knees and the other clap their hands or tap on a table.).*

2. **Two rows each:**
    Split the class in two halves. Group 1 plays/sings/claps two rows of an exercise and the other group takes the following two rows. Alternate the starting group. (You can choose to play one row per group as an alternative).

3. **Rhythm-relay, variation 1:**
    Each student plays/sings/claps **one bar each** in an exercise. Proceed clockwise in the group until the whole exercise is completed.

4. **Rhythm-relay, variation 2:**
    Each student plays/sings/claps **one row** in an exercise, next student continues with the next row, etc.

5. **Rhythm-relay, variation 3:**
    Make big signs with one rhythm-picture on each. Use rhythms from Basic Exercise 1A to begin with. (You can also add rhythms from Basic Exercise 1B). Let each student stand in a line, shoulder to shoulder, with a rhythm-sign in front of them. Start a beat or a metronome at approx. 80 BPM. The student to the far left starts to walk (to the pulse) in front of the others, singing the rhythm that each student is holding up. The student takes the last place and holds up his/her sign while the next student from left starts walking down the line.

6. **Canon:**
    Split the class in two (or more) and let each group start an exercise in Canon. You can choose the distance between the starting points. For instance, after 2, 4, 8 bars etc. *This trains the student to focus on their part while hearing other rhythms played at the same time.*

7. **Quad Libet:**
    Split the class in two. If the Exercise has two pages you can let one group play **page 1** and the other group **page 2** simultaneously. (Quad Libet). *This trains the student to focus on their part while hearing other rhythms played at the same time.*

Perhaps it's good to use a metronome or a steady beat while doing these exercises.

Tips for Jazz and Hip-Hop studies

Here are some tips for Jazz and Hip-Hop studies, or other triplet based music.

*   Play all exercises in chapter 1 with a jazz (triplet/swing) feel. Since chapter 1 is based on eighth notes, this will work fine.

*   Play the exercises in chapter 2 but swing the sixteenth notes to get some kind of Hip-Hop feel. Or why not Reggae!

Tips for Drums

The exercises in this book are excellent for drummers, and the most obvious way to use it is to play all exercises on a snare drum with alternating hands (left-right). But here are some suggestions on how to use the exercises for variation and coordination.

Drum exercise 1:

Snare:	Play the rhythms from chapter 1 - chapter 5
Kick:	Play the pulse (quarter notes), or another pattern

Drum exercise 2:

Snare:	Play the rhythms from chapter 1 - chapter 5
Kick:	Pulse (quarter notes), or another pattern
Ride:	Pulse (quarter notes)

Drum exercise 3:

Snare:	Play on beat 2 (& 4)
Kick:	Play on beat 1 (& 3), or another pattern
Ride/HiHat:	Play the exercises in chapter 1 and chapter 2

Drum exercise 4:

Snare (LH):	Play the first rhythm-picture in each bar in Ex. 3-1a - 3-2f
Snare (RH):	Play the second rhythm-picture in each bar in Ex. 3-1a - 3-2f *Switch starting hand.*

Drum exercise 5:

Snare:	Play the rhythms in chapter 5
Kick:	Pulse (quarter notes), or another pattern
Ride:	Pulse (quarter notes), or swing pattern
HiHat:	Play on beat 2

Drum exercise 6:

Snare:	Rim on beat (2 &) 4
Kick:	Play on beat 1 & 3 (or on beat 1, 2, 3, 4)
Ride:	Play the exercises in chapter 1 with a swing/jazz feel.

The Exercises for piano on pages 186-187 can also be played on percussion instruments. Play row 1 on, for example, a ride cymbal and row 2 on the snare simultaneously. This will improve the ability to read several systems at the same time.

I am sure you can find other ways to implement the exercises in this book into your drumming!

What you have learned

In chapter 14 you have:

- seen some examples on how to use this book with piano and drums and in ear training classes.

- seen som tips for jazz and hip-hop studies.

TEACHERS GUIDE

Teachers guide

Target group

This book is aimed to anyone who wants to develop their music sight-reading skills. Both professionals and beginners can take advantage of the methods and exercises in this book. If you are a beginner it is recommended that you work together with a music teacher. If you already know how to read music you can work with the book on your own.

The exercises work very well with all instruments including vocals and you can also use the book in ear training groups at music schools, for instance.

Perhaps the language style is aimed at students from 14 years and up. Still you can use it with younger students. It depends on their musical experience.

Goal

The goal of this book is to develop your ability to see written music, in this case rhythms, as pictures or words. This is the same principle as reading written text where you see word-pictures. You don't read letter by letter. Musicians that read music well see the notes in the same way.

Method

One important method used is the same as you would use when learning a new language: *listen – mimic – see.* When you learn a language, you learn it by ear. (If taught correctly). A teacher in french would say: Say after me please! – *un stylo.* Students reply: – *un stylo.* At the same time they see how to spell the word. Here, we use rhythms instead. Rhythm-pictures!

Teacher or no teacher

If you are a beginner at reading music, it is vital that you work with an experienced note-reader or music teacher. Since this book is built on learning by ear you need someone to guide you through the learning process. By doing this you will learn to read music in no time!

*If you can't find a teacher, you can at least find all the **Basic Exercises** <u>with audio</u> on our website: **www.khmp.se***

If you already know how to read music but just want to get better, more accurate, faster at reading, etc, you can work with this book on your own.

How to study

You should follow the study plan at the end of the book for a progressive development of your reading skills. The chapters are not written in a progressive order. Instead, each chapter develops its own topic. Meaning that *the start of chapter 2 is easier than the end of chapter 1.* So, you should **not** read this book from start to end. Instead follow the study plan thoroughly! By doing this you will also encounter explanatory texts when you need them.

Methodologies

What other methods are being used in this book to benefit your learning process? Well, there are many but here are the most important ones:

1. **Repetition** – Most of the exercises are built on repetition and structure. If you for instance go to pages 14-15, where you find Exercise 1a, you will find that this exercise methodically goes through the eight rhythms presented in Basic Exercise 1A. The first eight bars start with rhythm A followed by rhythms B-H in the following way: A+A, A+B, A+C, A+D, A+E, A+F, A+G, A+H. Then you start with rhythm B: B+A, B+B, B+C etc until you have gone through all eight rhythms from Basic Exercise 1A. The idea is that you must repeat and repeat until the rhythms are stuck in your subconscious mind and just pop up when reading. Most exercises in this book follow this principle.

2. **Musicality** – Since we repeat every rhythm many times, musical phrases with various themes will emerge. The opposite would be random rhythms – which is not very musical.

3. **From shorter note values to longer** – Traditionally, music theory or when learning to read music, tend to start with longer note values, like half notes, whole notes or perhaps quarter notes, and move gradually to shorter ones. In this book it is the opposite. You start with shorter note values, like eighth notes or sixteenth notes and move towards longer note values. This will enhance the rhythmic sense by automatically using subdivisions on all note values.
    It's a fact that children more easily read eighth notes than half notes. Or ask yourself; what is easier: eighth note triplets or half note triplets?
    You will definitely think eighth note triplets!

4. **Made for reading several staffs simultaneously** – If you look closely at the exercises, you will note that the spacing between notes sometimes look strange or wide. This is on purpose.
    The staffs are meant to be read simultaneously if you want to practice that. For instance, if you play keyboards, then you can play one staff with the right hand and one with the left hand. All notes will fall correctly under the right beat or subdivision of a beat. See pages 186-187 for more on this.

5. **Music instead of math** – Written music is very mathematical. Like: *four 16th-notes equals one 1/4-note.* In this book we don't discuss the theory and mathematical approach to notes that much. Instead, we use ear training and musicality to learn how to read. *It is still good to know the math behind rhythms so I encourage you to get hold of a good music theory book. Also see the Appendix at the end of this book.*

6. **Seeing music notes as pictures** – Lastly, I once more want to point out that we read by pictures. Both regular text but also music notes! That is why I often use the word **rhythm-pictures** instead of just **rhythms** in this book.

Contact information

If you have any questions, please let me know!

You can contact me through e-mail:

info@khmp.se

Website: www.khmp.se

STUDY PLAN

Study plan

This is a study plan that will fit most students, but your tutor may have other suggestions. There is no time allotted to the study plan so you can study at your own pace. *Exercises in italics are supplementary studies and can be completed some time during the step that follows.*

	X	Chapter	Assignments	Pages
STEP I	☐	Introduction	Read the Introduction	6-7
	☐	Teachers guide.	Read the Teachers guide and Methodologies section	192-193
	☐	Ch. 1	8th-notes, 4/4-time, **Basic Exercise 1A**, Exercise 1a	10-15
	☐	Ch. 2	16th-notes, 2/4-time, **Basic Exercise 2A**, Exercise 2a	38-43
	☐	Ch. 3	16th-notes & 8th-notes, 3/4-time, Exercise 3-1a	64-67
	☐	Ch. 3	8th-notes & 16th-notes, 3/4-time, Exercise 3-2a	74-77
	☐	*Ch. 3*	*16th-notes, 3/4-time, Exercise 3-3a*	*84-87*
	☐	*Ch. 4*	*8th-notes, 16th-notes, 4/4-time, Exercise 4-1a*	*92-95*

Check the box when finished with the assignment, so you can follow your progression.

	X	Chapter	Assignments	Pages
STEP II	☐	Ch. 1	8th-notes, Rests, **Basic Exercise 1B** and Exercise 1b	16-19
	☐	Ch. 2	16th-notes, Rests, **Basic Exercise 2B**, and Exercise 2b	44-47
	☐	Ch. 1	Exercise 1d	24-25
	☐	Ch. 2	Exercise 2d	50-51
	☐	Ch. 3	Exercise 3-1b	68-69
	☐	Ch. 3	Exercise 3-2b	78-79
	☐	Ch. 3	Exercise 3-2d	80-81
	☐	Ch. 3	Exercise 3-1d	70-71
	☐	Ch. 1	Exercise 1f	28-29
	☐	Ch. 2	Exercise 2f	54-55
	☐	Ch. 4	Exercise 4-1d	98-99
	☐	*Ch. 3*	*Exercise 3-1f*	*72-73*
	☐	*Ch. 3*	*Exercise 3-2f*	*82-83*
	☐	*Ch. 4*	*Exercise 4-1b*	*96-97*
	☐	*Ch. 4*	*Exercise 4-1f*	*100-101*
	☐	*Ch. 3*	*Exercise 3-3b*	*88-89*

Note:
*Alll **Basic Exercises** can be found with audio on our website: www.khmp.se*

	X	Chapter	Assignments	Pages
STEP III	☐	Ch. 1	Ties, 4/4-time, Exercise 1c	20-23
	☐	Ch. 2	Exercise 2c	48-49
	☐	Ch. 1	Exercise 1e	26-27
	☐	Ch. 2	Exercise 2e	52-53
	☐	*Ch. 3*	*Exercise 3-1c (your own excercise, see pg. 65) .... copy pages 66-67*	
	☐	*Ch. 3*	*Exercise 3-2c (your own excercise, see pg. 75)........ copy pages 76-77*	
	☐	*Ch. 4*	*Exercise 4-1c (your own excercise, see pg. 93)........ copy pages 94-95*	
	☐	*Ch. 3*	*Exercise 3-3c (your own excercise, see pg. 85)........ copy pages 86-87*	

	X	Chapter	Assignments	Pages
STEP IV	☐	Ch. 5	8th-note triplets, **Basic Exercise 5A**, Exercise 5a	104-107
	☐	Ch. 6	16th-note triplets, **Basic Exercise 6A**, Exercise 6a	118-119
	☐	Ch. 5	8th-note triplets, Rests, **Basic Exercise 5B**, Exercise 5b	107-109
	☐	Ch. 6	16th-note triplets, Rests, **Basic Exercise 6B**, Exercise 6b	120
	☐	Ch. 5	Exercise 5d	110
	☐	Ch. 6	Exercise 6d	121
	☐	Ch. 5	Exercise 5f	111
	☐	Ch. 6	Exercise 6f	121
	☐	Ch. 5	Exercise 5c	109
	☐	Ch. 5	Exercise 5e and 5g	110-111
	☐	Ch. 5	Quarter note triplets, Triplet study #1-2, Exercise 5c alt. 2	112-114
	☐	*Ch. 6*	*Exercises 6c,6e och 6g (your own excercise, see pg. 119)..... copy page 119*	

Note: Go back to earlier exercises regularly for repetition!

Study plan cont.

X	Chapter	Assignments	Pages

Note: Go back to earlier exercises regularly for repetition!

Note values

Whole note *Semibreve*	
Half notes *Minim*	
Quarter notes *Crotchet*	
Eighth notes *Quaver*	
Sixteenth notes *Semiquaver*	
32nd notes *Demisemiquaver*	

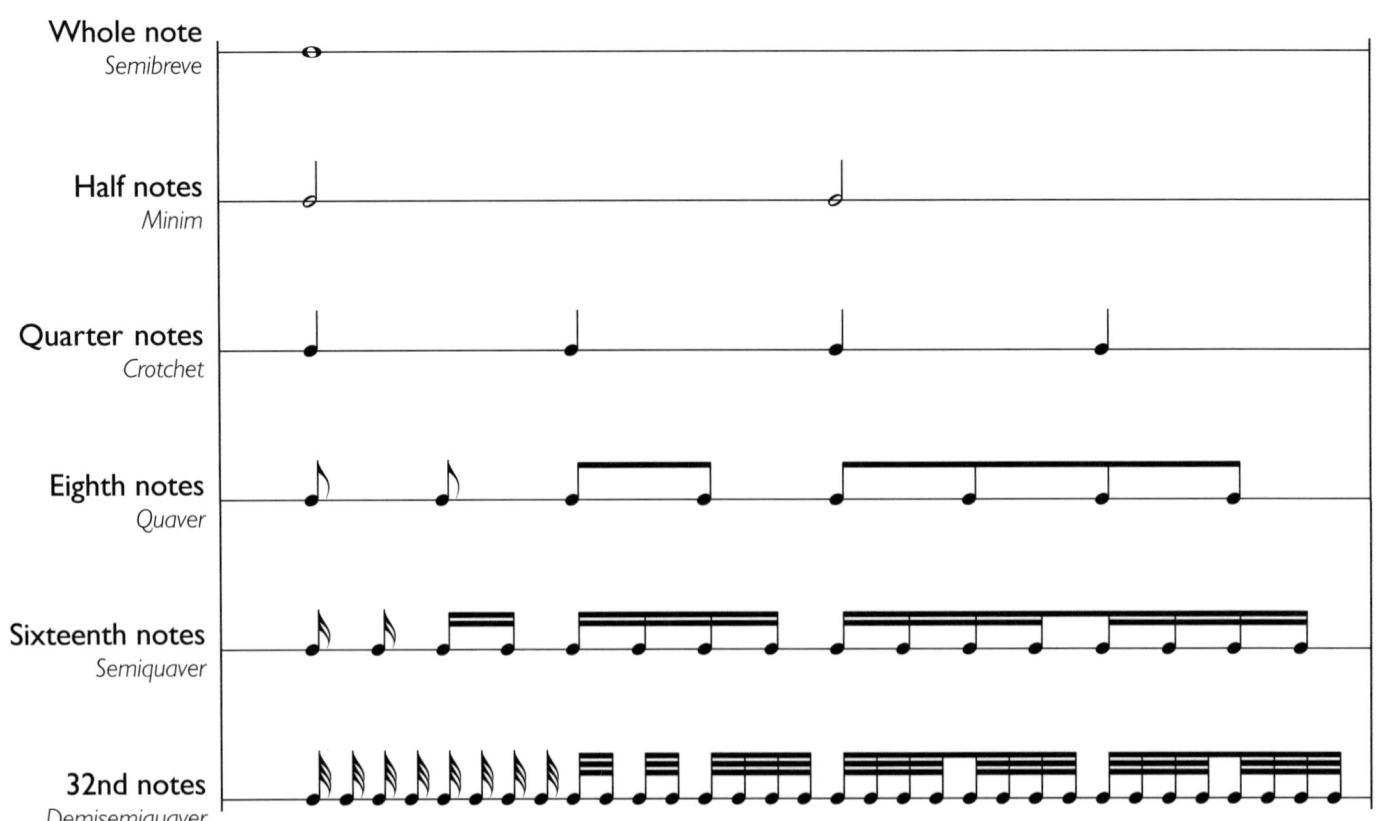

Rests

****Whole rest** *Semibreve rest*	
Half rest *Minim rest*	
Quarter rest *Crotchet rest*	
Eighth rest *Quaver rest*	
Sixteenth rest *Semiquaver rest*	
32nd rest *Demisemiquaver rest*	

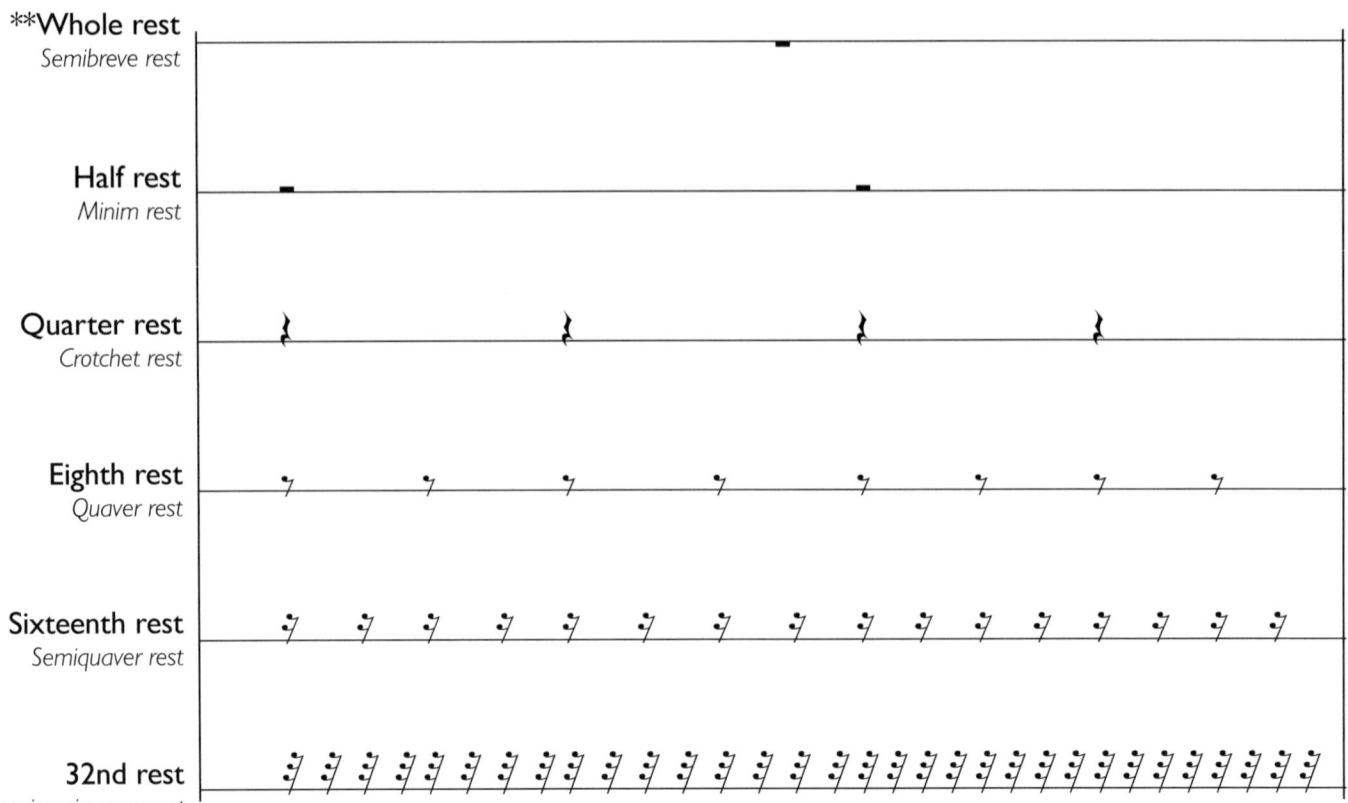

*** A Whole rest is valid for a whole bar no matter what time signature
(with a few exceptions). It is usually placed in the middle of the bar.*

Note grid

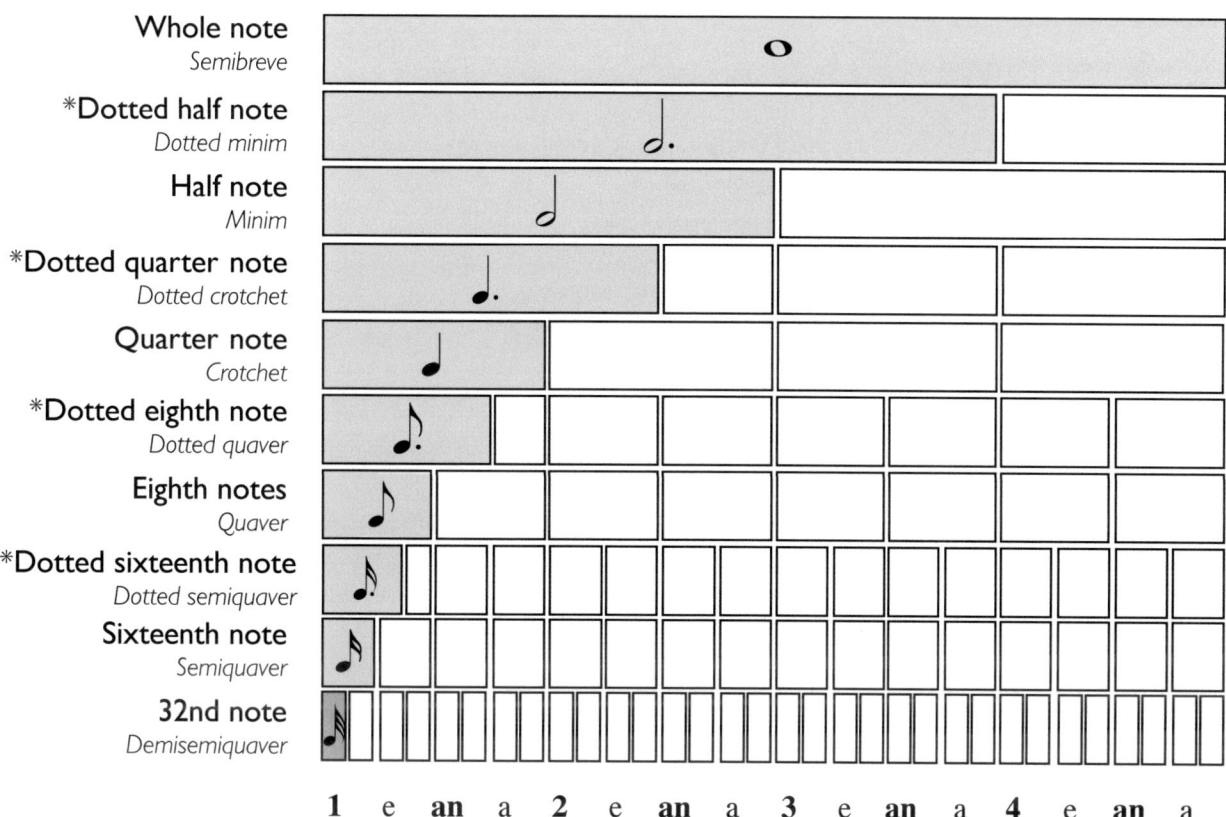

Whole note
Semibreve

***Dotted half note**
Dotted minim

Half note
Minim

***Dotted quarter note**
Dotted crotchet

Quarter note
Crotchet

***Dotted eighth note**
Dotted quaver

Eighth notes
Quaver

***Dotted sixteenth note**
Dotted semiquaver

Sixteenth note
Semiquaver

32nd note
Demisemiquaver

1 e **an** a **2** e **an** a **3** e **an** a **4** e **an** a

* Placing a dot to the right of a notehead lengthens the note's duration by one half. *You can read more about dotted notes on page 183.*

Thanks to:

...my dear friend **Anders Wihk** for helping me with the English language!

Check out Anders' super trio under the name **SAME TREE DIFFERENT FRUIT** playing cool and jazzy arrangements of ABBA songs:

Anders Wihk – piano, arrangements
Steve Gadd – drums
Svante Henryson – bass

And with guest appeareances by:

Robben Ford – guitar
David Sanborn – saxophone

The music is available on iTunes and Spotify etc.

For more info go to www.sametreedifferentfruit.com